CEOs Featured in *Dare to Lead!*

- Roger Berkowitz, CEO of **Legal Seafoods**
- Gert Boyle, chairman of **Columbia Sportswear**
- Doug Dayton, founding CEO of **Target**
- Dave Duffield, founder and chairman of **PeopleSoft**
- Chris Emery and Larry Finnson, cofounders of **Chris and Larry's Clodhoppers**
- Dan Firestone, cofounder and CEO of **Somera**
- Dale Fuller, chairman and CEO of **Borland**
- Bill George, former chairman and CEO of **Medtronic**
- Dave Gold, founder and CEO of **99 Cents Only**
- Mitchell Gold, founder and CEO of **Mitchell Gold Furniture**
- Gary Hoover, founder and CEO of **BookStop** and **Hoover's Financial**
- Wayne Inouye, CEO, **eMachines** and **Gateway**
- Ron Joyce, cofounder and CEO of **Tim Hortons**
- Jim Koch, founder and CEO of **The Boston Beer Co.**
- John LaMacchia, CEO of **Cincinnati Bell** and **Tellme Networks**
- Sheldon Laube, founder and CEO of **Centerbeam**
- John McAdam, president and CEO of **F5 Networks**
- Jim McCann, founder and CEO of **1-800-FLOWERS**
- David Neeleman, founder and chairman of **JetBlue**
- Marilyn Carlson Nelson, CEO of **Carlson Companies**
- John Osher, founder and CEO of **SpinBrush**
- Larry Page, cofounder and former CEO of **Google**
- Lawrence Perlman, former chairman and CEO of **Control Data/Ceridian**
- John Shields, former chairman and CEO of **Trader Joe's**
- Bob Stiller, founder and CEO of **Green Mountain Coffee Roasters**
- Albert Straus, CEO of **Straus Family Creamery**
- Bill Sweedler, chairman and CEO of **Joe Boxer**
- Richard Tait, cofounder and CEO of **Cranium**
- Rich Teerlink, former chairman and CEO of **Harley-Davidson**
- Peter Thiel, founder and former CEO of **PayPal**
- Victor Tsao, cofounder and CEO of **Linksys**
- Jeannette White, founder and CEO of **Sytel**
- Carol H. Williams, founder and CEO of **Carol H. Williams Advertising**

- Mary Kay Ash, founder and CEO of **Mary Kay, Inc.**
- Gordon Bethune, former chairman and CEO of **Continental Airlines**
- August Busch III, chairman of **Anheuser-Busch**
- Ely Callaway, former chairman and CEO of **Callaway Golf**
- Emma Chappell, founder and former CEO of **United Bank of Philadelphia**
- Scott Cook, founder and CEO of **Intuit**
- Fred DeLuca, founder and CEO of **Subway**
- Brian Devine, CEO of **PETCO**
- Carlos Ghosn, chairman and CEO of **Nissan**
- Stelios Haji-Ioannou, founder and former CEO of **easyJet**
- Steve Jobs, CEO of **Pixar**
- Bob Johnson, founder and former CEO of **BET**
- John H. Johnson, founder and chairman of **Johnson Publishing**
- Sheryl Leach, founder and CEO of **Lyrick**
- Scott Livengood, CEO of **Krispy Kreme**
- Bernie Marcus and Arthur Blank, cofounders of **Home Depot**
- Jeff McClelland, president and COO of **America West**
- Paul Otellani, president and COO of **Intel**
- John Peterman, founder and CEO of **J. Peterman Co.**
- Howard Schultz, founder and former CEO of **Starbucks**
- Ron Shaich, founder and CEO of **Panera Bread**
- Jim Sinegal, founder and CEO of **Costco**
- Fred Smith, founder and chairman of **FedEx**
- Esther Snyder, cofounder, chairman, and CEO of **In-N-Out Burger**
- Chris Sullivan, founder and CEO of **Outback Steakhouse**
- Sam Walton, founder and former CEO of **Wal-Mart**

DARE! TO LEAD!

Uncommon Sense
AND
Unconventional Wisdom
From 50 Top CEOs

By

Mike Merrill

CAREER
PRESS
Franklin Lakes, NJ

DARE TO LEAD!
EDITED BY KRISTEN PARKES
TYPESET BY EILEEN DOW MUNSON
Cover design by DesignConcept
Printed in the U.S.A. by Book-mart Press

To order this title, please call toll-free 1-800-CAREER-1 (NJ and Canada: 201-848-0310) to order using VISA or MasterCard, or for further information on books from Career Press.

The Career Press, Inc., 3 Tice Road, PO Box 687,
Franklin Lakes, NJ 07417
www.careerpress.com

Library of Congress Cataloging-in-Publication Data

Merrill, Mike, 1962-
    Dare to lead! : uncommon sense and unconventional wisdom from 50 top CEOs / by Mike Merrill.
        p. cm.
    Includes bibliographical references and index.
    ISBN 1-56414-752-5 (paper)
    1. Leadership. 2. Executive ability. 3. Chief executive officers. 4. Industrial management. I. Title.

HD57.7.M468 2004
658.4′092--dc22

                                                                    2004045851

For the men and women in uniform,

who put their lives on the line every day

to make the world a better place.

Acknowledgments

Although writing is an individual sport, creating a book truly is a team effort. I couldn't have done it without help from many contributors.

Special thanks to Erica Angyal, for editing countless drafts, providing moral support, and cracking the whip throughout the process. I received invaluable support and assistance from: my parents, COL (Ret.) and Mrs. Will G. Merrill, Jr.; CAPT (Ret.) James Mathews, USN; COL Will G. Merrill, Jr. (Ret.); Lynn Klar; Mary Merrill; Deborah Rogers; and Wolfgang Angyal. Without their help, this book would not have gotten out of the starting gate.

I'm also indebted to all the leaders who took the time to share their stories and offer advice and wisdom, including: Doug Dayton, founding CEO of Target; David Neeleman, founder and chairman of JetBlue; Marilyn Carlson Nelson, CEO of Carlson Companies; Larry Page, cofounder and former CEO of Google; Rich Teerlink, former chairman and CEO of Harley-Davidson; Jim McCann, founder and CEO of 1-800-FLOWERS; Bill Sweedler, chairman and CEO of Windsong Allegiance/JOE BOXER; Dale Fuller, chairman and CEO of Borland; Jeannette White, founder and CEO of Sytel; Dave Duffield, founder and chairman of PeopleSoft; Lawrence Perlman, former chairman and CEO of Control Data/Ceridian; Bill George, former chairman and CEO of Medtronic; Dave Gold, founder and CEO of 99 Cents Only; John Shields, former chairman and CEO of Trader Joe's; Wayne Inouye, CEO of eMachines and Gateway; Victor Tsao, cofounder and CEO of Linksys; Bob Stiller, founder and CEO of Green Mountain Coffee Roasters; John McAdam, president and CEO of F5 Networks; Richard Tait, cofounder and CEO of Cranium; Gert Boyle, chairman and former CEO of Columbia Sportswear; Peter Thiel, founder and former CEO of PayPal; Carol H. Williams, founder and CEO of Carol H. Williams; Mitchell Gold, founder and CEO of Mitchell Gold Furniture; Albert Straus, CEO of Straus Family Creamery; Jim Koch, founder and CEO, The Boston Beer Co.; Roger Berkowitz, CEO of Legal Seafoods; Bob Stiller, founder and CEO of Green Mountain Coffee Company; John LaMacchia, CEO of Cincinnati Bell and Tellme Networks; Ron Joyce, cofounder and CEO of Tim Hortons; Gary Hoover, founder and CEO of BookStop and Hoover's Financial; Chris Emery and Larry Finnson, cofounders of Chris & Larry's Clodhoppers; Dan Firestone, cofounder and CEO of Somera; Sheldon Laube, founder and CEO of Centerbeam; John Osher, founder and CEO of SpinBrush; and Phi Schlein, former CEO of Macy's. All these leaders are extremely busy, and it takes a special kind of person to selflessly give his or her time so others may benefit. Thank you.

In addition to interviewing CEOs, I got valuable information and insights from additional interviews with: Melinda Sowers, Richard Luna, and Kagee Tate, Outback Steakhouse; David Crosswhite, Strategos; Cindy McCaffrey, Google; Jill Birnbaum and Rachel Jacobs, 99 Cents Only; Shirley Roberts, Mitchell Gold Company; Wolfgang Angyal, Reidel; and Joe Cooper, International Association of Machinists.

Interviewing a large group of CEOs is not a task to be undertaken lightly. Many thanks to everyone who helped arrange interviews, including: Colette Landi Sipperly, Windsong Allegiance/JOE BOXER; Cindy McCaffrey and Raymond Nasr, Google; Gareth Edmondson-Jones, JetBlue; Tom Patterson, Weston Presidio; Anita Mast, Clarium Capital; Achilles Armenakis, Auburn University; Karen Sohl, Linksys/Cisco Systems; Diane Davis and Rick Pizer, Green Mountain Coffee Roasters; Safiya Umoja and Shirley Priestly, Carol H. Williams Advertising; Doug Cody, Carlson Companies; Alane Moran, F5 Networks; Denise Chastain and Yvonne Pendleton, Mary Kay Cosmetics; Kris Comtois, Boston Beer Company; Holly Hagerman, Connect Public Relations; Ken Young, 1-800-FLOWERS; Rick Havacko and Mike Kilroy, Maples Communication; Joan Giblin and Ann Flannery, Legal Seafoods; Kim Schamp, Columbia Sportswear; Marci Gottlieb, TellMe Networks; Eloise Goldman, Mitchell Gold Company; Vivien Straus, Straus Family Creamery; Dave Gold and Albert Lee, 99 Cents Only. Special thanks to Lawrence Moon, Lee Wright, Laura Rippy, Mary Merrill, Will Merrill, Kathy Yonge, Lina Ingraham, Deborah Rogers, and Joe Cecin for their help in securing interviews. Thanks also to Cassie Maas for providing invaluable technical support, Dennis Shepherd for graphic design help, and Susan and Nick Tsantes for helping point me in the right direction.

Thanks also to my agent, Michael Larsen, and Michael Pye, Michael Lewis, Kristen Parkes, Kirsten Beucler, and the whole team at Career Press.

Contents

Chapter 1

Lead From the Front

One of the most stirring examples of leadership in recent years came out of the tragic terrorist attacks on September 11, 2001. Among the hundreds of firefighters who died were the top five senior members of the New York Fire Department. All five were leading the evacuation from the front lines—not directing the rescue from the safety of a remote command post. Within that terrible tragedy was a stirring example of leadership under fire.

The very first thing people learn in the military is that you lead from the front. The motto of the infantry is "Follow Me," not "Hey, guys, you go charge the hill while I stay behind." This principle is just as true in business. It doesn't take long for employees to figure out if leaders aren't practicing what they are preaching. When the boss is spending lavishly, it sends a silent signal to everyone else that they don't have to worry about expenses. The "do as I say, not as I do" mentality is bound to fail.

Lead by Example

It's not uncommon for JetBlue customers to encounter David Neeleman issuing boarding passes, loading baggage, or handing out biscotti onboard the aircraft. What makes it unusual is that David is the CEO of JetBlue. Instead of staying safely ensconced in his office, David prefers to be out chatting with his customers face to face. He makes a point of flying on a JetBlue flight at least once a week, which gives him a chance to interact with both employees and customers.

When other airline CEOs were raising ticket prices, wringing concessions out of shell-shocked unions, and begging the government for loans, David was issuing boarding passes, loading baggage, and handing out biscotti to grateful customers. By working side by side with the flight crews and listening to suggestions and complaints from customers, he sends a powerful message to JetBlue employees: what they're doing is important. How can flight attendants complain about cleaning the plane when the CEO is on his hands and knees working beside them? Equally important, they know that *he knows* what they have to do.

Although he introduces himself and gives a little speech on every flight he works, David doesn't rely on showmanship. Instead, he tries to talk to every customer on the flight personally. He also spends time chatting with the flight crews, thanking them for what they're doing, and letting them know that they're important. By spending one day a week letting customers and employees know they're important, David reinforces the vision and sets the character of the company.

Skeptics might say that one person can't possibly make a difference in a company that large. After all, if you do the math, there's no way David could talk to *every* employee, let alone every customer, and still have time to run the company. Although he can't personally talk to every flight attendant, pilot, and mechanic, the people he does talk to spread the word.

"I'm never going to fly with every one of them. Not at this rate, because they're growing faster than I can fly with them," David says. "But every one of them knows that I fly on the planes, and every one of them knows that I vacuum airplanes and that I get on my hands and knees and pick up garbage. And every one of our reservations agents has talked to someone who has been on a plane with me. And they know that it's important to me."[1]

But is that the CEO's role? Doesn't the boss have better things to do than worry about little things like that? Maybe not, if you believe that leaders set the tone for the rest of the organization. Sydney Finkelstein, professor of management at Dartmouth's Tuck School of Business and author of *Why Smart Executives Fail*, calls it setting the moral compass of the company. "When the culture is wrong, it permeates the entire organization and reaches so far down that it can take years to hear the other shoe drop," Finkelstein explains. "In the absence of clear guidelines on what is appropriate and inappropriate, some people might push the envelope too far."[2]

Live the Example

Whether your company has five employees or 5,000, the leaders set the tone for everyone else in the organization. Bernie Marcus and Arthur Blank built Home Depot into an industry leader by constantly reinforcing the message that the customer comes first. The two cofounders were legendary for showing up unannounced for "store walks" with their associates. "This is a people business, and our goal is anything from engaging them in a strategic conversation to just getting to know each other so we can transfer culture and ideas," Arthur explains. "It's about building relationships so people are open to learning; it's about creating a teachable moment."[3]

Even when the company was doing $30 billion in revenues, Bernie and Arthur started and ended each weeklong training class for store managers. When the company grew too large to personally interact with each of the employees, they broadcast a weekly television show to every store called *Breakfast with Bernie and Arthur* to talk to employees, build morale, and keep associates informed about what was going on in the company.[4] "We set the stage. When you start handing it off to people who do it professionally, you don't get the same emotion, the same direction, because we are the 'they' when people say, 'This is what they believe.' And they have to hear it from our mouths."[5]

After the two founders retired from Home Depot, Arthur bought the Atlanta Falcons, where he applied the same leadership principles to lead a professional sports team. It was apparent pretty quickly that he wasn't a typical NFL owner when he showed up at training camp and slept in a dorm room at Furman University, just like one of the players. "I want to learn what I can do to make things better," Arthur said. "The players and coaches are most important. I just walk from room to room, drop down in a chair, and listen to what they have to say." At the opening practice, he took the field in shorts and a sweatshirt, watching firsthand to learn and ask questions.[6]

Arthur spread the same gospel he preached at Home Depot: it's all about the customer. "I've told all of our people, from management to the concessionaires, the fans own this house, and we need to treat them with as much care, love, and affection as possible."[7] When star quarterback Michael Vick was injured the following year and the team lost several consecutive games, Arthur publicly apologized to Falcons fans. Sooner or later every team has a bad season, but you don't find many team owners with the courage to stand up and take responsibility for it.

Actions Speak Louder Than Words

You have to live the message that you're conveying or people will see through it in a heartbeat. Doug Dayton, the founding CEO of Target, spent most of his time in stores, stock rooms, or on loading docks—not in the executive suite. Like Bernie and Arthur at Home Depot, Doug set the tone for the rest of the organization. Working side by side in the trenches also gave him a much better view of what was going on inside the stores. Like David Neeleman getting direct feedback from customers, Doug saw firsthand where Target needed to improve. You can't get that kind of perspective relying on reports from other people. Equally as important, his direct involvement let his employees know he was down in the trenches working with them.

When 99 Cents Only employees see Dave Gold picking up trash in the parking lot, it sends a message that no amount of pronouncements from the human resources department can touch. Even though he's on the *Forbes* 400 list of wealthiest Americans, Dave is usually the first one in the office every morning. Even though he has a team of experienced buyers, he still works side by side with them, teaching, coaching, and looking for the next great bargain. If you spend time with Dave's employees, it's immediately obvious that they love working with him. As the leader, Dave's example sends a message that clearly inspires the rest of the company.

Live Your Ideals

Leading by example means living by your principles in everything you do. When Marilyn Carlson Nelson was on the board of Northwestern Bell, now part of Qwest, the company ran into an unusual problem.

As the company grew, it hired and trained the brightest managers to travel throughout the region to work with major customers. Despite the fact that they were working for a blue-chip company, the managers who were women and minorities weren't allowed to participate in the Rotary Club. When Hank McConnell, Northwestern Bell's CEO, threatened to pull the Bell system support for civic organizations that wouldn't accept women and minorities, several board members had a fit. "You can't do that! You can't put it at risk. This is not the time," they cried.

"When is the time?" Hank responded. He went to the mat, ruffling feathers at the Rotary Club—and on his own board—to fight for his employees.[8] Hank prevailed and the Rotary Club changed its rules, opening doors that had been previously closed solely on the basis of gender or race. "My uncle ran away to marry my aunt, because my grandmother wouldn't accept her into the family because she was Catholic and they were Protestant," Marilyn said. "There are probably just as many examples today that will seem just as silly tomorrow. You just need to open your eyes to them."[9]

When Marilyn became CEO of Carlson Companies, she took the responsibility to heart, living and leading by her ideals. With brands such as TGI Friday's, Radisson Hotels, Carlson Travel Network, and the Thomas Cook Group, Carlson Companies has 190,000 employees worldwide. Although there were plenty of women and minorities in line for senior management positions, Marilyn noticed that very few of them were actually promoted when executive positions became available. In each case, the reasoning was that the individual didn't have a particular skill set necessary for that position.

Although it was a valid explanation, Marilyn didn't let the issue drop. She knew that people who needed finance skills could get finance training. "Instead of coming right up to the night before and having someone say, 'Well, she is not very good at financials,' or 'He's not a good communicator,' we try to identify those things early." Marilyn instituted a leadership development program to give upcoming managers the depth and breadth of skills they might need as they moved up in the organization. She also got the company involved in a mentoring program, matching up middle-level managers with mentors in different companies.[10]

The results were inspiring. Today, 40 percent of the senior managers at Carlson Companies are women or minorities. Equally important, the quality of leadership has improved as middle-level managers and senior executives gained a broader set of skills. "We have to hold ourselves accountable," Marilyn said. "Every single one of us is competing with the best minds around the world. Today, the smart brains are being applied around the world. Believe it or not, they don't come in any one color or race or sexual preference."[11]

You Can't Lead From the Rear

You can't inspire an organization by sitting in your office writing memos and press releases. In too many businesses, this fundamental principle of leadership is often overlooked. The only way to effectively lead an organization is to live by the example you're preaching. By relentlessly reinforcing the message that customers come first, Bernie and Arthur built Home Depot into a $30-billion company. Doug Dayton also led from the front lines as he guided Target into an industry leader. When other airlines were under fire, David Neeleman's example inspired his employees and delighted his customers as JetBlue ascended to the rank of most profitable airline in the country—in a single year.

Advertising guru Carol Williams said it best: "There are a lot of people in corporate America that really don't understand that there is a difference between leading and managing. You manage paper, you lead people."[12]

Chapter 2

When the Going Gets Tough, Go Around

Taking on a well-entrenched competitor can be a quick road to disaster. One of the tried-and-true principles in the military is to bypass pockets of resistance. Throughout history, armies have won decisive victories by outflanking their opponents instead of launching bloody frontal attacks. It's a lot easier—and much less costly in the long run—to simply go around, reinforce your strengths, and leave pockets of opposition to mop up later.

The same principle holds true in business. When you run into well-entrenched competitors, don't try to attack head on. Instead, focus on areas your competitors have neglected or ignored. In many cases, bypassing the opposition is much more effective, giving you a way around the competition without launching a costly frontal assault.

Sam Walton was famous for avoiding big cities in the early days of Wal-Mart, only opening stores in towns with fewer than 35,000 people. His reasoning had nothing to do with marketing studies or consumer preferences. He was far more practical—he avoided cities with populations of more than 35,000 simply because that was JCPenney's threshold for opening stores. By staying in small towns for years, he avoided competing with JCPenney, and later Kmart, almost entirely. Wal-Mart grew larger, and eventually amassed enough buying power to compete directly in its own right. If he had taken on JCPenney from the outset, Wal-Mart's history would be completely different.

Dan Firestone, founder and CEO of Somera, did much the same thing, but he avoided competitors on two fronts. While he recognized that selling telecommunications equipment to corporate customers was a lucrative market, he was concerned that fewer barriers to entry in the enterprise market would quickly turn the equipment into a commodity. Instead, he decided to focus on the smaller, but potentially more lucrative market of telecom infrastructure, selling higher ticket, more complex equipment to carriers.

On the flip side, Lucent, Nortel, Cisco, and other industry goliaths were slugging it out over the telecom infrastructure market. Knowing that would be a tough fight, Dan steered his company toward the less glamorous—and often overlooked—area of used telecommunications equipment. Although used switches aren't as sexy as brand-new equipment, Somera had much less competition—and accordingly, higher margins.

By avoiding the competitive enterprise market completely, and then steering clear of the big guys in the carrier market, he exploited a void in the marketplace and built Somera into a $200-million telecommunications company.[1] Like Sam Walton avoiding JCPenney, if Dan had tried to take on Nortel and Lucent on their own turf, it likely would have been a drastically different outcome.

Oh, Thank Heaven for 7-Eleven!

When Joe Coloumbe started Pronto Markets in southern California in 1958, convenience stores were still relatively new at the time. He built a modestly successful business and was slowly, but steadily, growing the company. In 1967, while on a business trip in Dallas, he saw the first 7-Eleven stores. He knew instantly he was in trouble. Not only were the 7-Eleven stores nicer than his Pronto Markets, with more products and lower prices, but Southland Corporation, 7-Eleven's owner, had very deep pockets. Despite his enthusiasm for his own creation, he knew that Pronto Markets would be in trouble when 7-Eleven expanded to California. That, he figured, was only a matter of time.

As he was casting about for new ideas, Joe saw two trends converging. Prior to World War II, only 1 percent of Americans were college graduates. With the GI Bill, more people than ever before were graduating from college, leading to a more educated population. The second trend was the rise of the commercial airliner, which meant that exotic locations were no longer out of reach. People could now travel to places they'd only dreamed about, exposing them to new cultures and foods. Joe thought, "If I can fashion something that will respond to both of those, I've got something." He knew that to compete successfully with 7-Eleven, Pronto Markets had to become more than a convenience store, tap into an educated population, and exploit the romance and excitement of exploring new cultures. Joe steered around the competition from 7-Eleven, transforming Pronto Markets into a brand-new concept. He called it Trader Joe's.

To capture the romance and charm of traveling to exotic places, Joe decked out his stores with cedar planks and created a homespun nautical theme. The store manager (Captain), the assistant manager (First Mate), and the crewmembers all wore colorful Hawaiian shirts. He also started an innovative merchandising tactic. Instead of selling the same products at the same prices, Joe sought out exceptional bargains, and then bought as much as he could get his hands on.

While the typical convenience store carried staples such as milk, bread, and candy, Trader Joe's initially carried an eclectic variety of merchandise, including women's hosiery, ammunition, and phonograph records. By the time he adopted his new identity, Trader Joe's looked nothing like the original Pronto Markets, and 7-Eleven no longer looked like a threat.

During the 1970s, Joe got into the wine business, continuing his strategy of searching for great values and then buying large quantities. Following the same approach, he later expanded into food in the 1980s. The company grew along with its merchandise, and Trader Joe's evolved into an upscale food and wine specialty store with bargain prices.

In 1987, Joe recruited his friend and Stanford fraternity brother John Shields to take over as CEO. John had been unofficially involved with Trader Joe's from the beginning, helping his business school classmate write the original business plan. When he took the helm, John saw another industry trend on the horizon—downward pressure on prices.

As Trader Joe's navigated upstream to avoid 7-Eleven, it gradually sailed into direct competition with supermarkets. Although Wal-Mart hadn't yet begun selling groceries, new superstores such as Price Club and Costco were offering wholesale prices to customers buying larger volumes. Trader Joe's was already offering great prices; it was only a matter of time before margins were impacted as well. Recognizing the threat headed their way, John steered Trader Joe's around the competition once again.

Having spent a lot of time in London, John regularly shopped at Marks & Spencer, a famous British department store that was 100 percent private label. "I thought, 'My God, these guys have really got it,'" John said. He took a page out of their book, making a concerted effort to increase the number of private-label products at Trader Joe's.[2]

Under John's direction, private labels went from a handful of products at Trader Joe's to the centerpiece of the company's strategy. Today, 85 percent of the items that Trader Joe's sells are private label (the other 15 percent is wine and beer), compared to 14 percent private label in supermarkets.[3] Furthermore, the "generic" brands in the supermarkets are usually sold on the same shelf as the brand-name items. Trader Joe's products carry colorful names such as Trader Giotto's, Trader Jacque's, and Trader Ming's, reinforcing its unique identity. Private labels also took the pressure off their food suppliers, who were criticized by the supermarkets for selling to Trader Joe's too cheaply.[4]

Trader Joe's not only still follows its original charter of offering upscale specialty food at lower-than-average prices, but it's turned it into an art form. Teams of buyers travel the world looking for great buys, still capturing the essence of the mystery and charm of faraway places that Joe Coloumbe originally envisioned. The company cut costs by having buyers work directly with hundreds of suppliers worldwide. "It took a lot of investment in terms of working with vendors and developing products and things like that, but it really pays off," John explained. "It also gives you a protected position in the marketplace."[5]

While establishing its own unique identity, Trader Joe's evolved into a culinary treasure hunt. Some competitively priced staples are always in stock, and some vary depending on the season, or simply the availability. At any point in time, customers may find garlic naan, artichoke antipasto, or raspberry salsa. The typical Trader Joe's store carries about 2,500 products, compared to 25,000 or more at the average supermarket.[6] The goal is to carry only high-quality products it can get at a great price. If it can't sell the product cheaper than the supermarkets, Trader Joe's doesn't carry it. After all, if it's not adding value, why bother?

By avoiding a fight with 7-Eleven, Joe Coloumbe transformed Pronto Markets into Trader Joe's, expanding the concept as he expanded the company. John Shields later steered around the competition once again, expanding the private-label line into what is now Trader Joe's signature. At the same time, he grew the company from 27 stores on the West Coast to 174 nationwide by the time he handed over the wheel 10 years later, growing sales from $132 million to $2 billion. Although Trader Joe's is a private company and doesn't release sales figures, competitors estimate Trader Joe's stores average $1,000 per square foot each year, double that of conventional supermarkets and more than triple that of most specialty food stores.[7] Many factors contributed to its success, but navigating around the competition played a key role in building Trader Joe's unique identity and cultivating its loyal following.

Tiptoe Quietly Around Your Competition

Steering clear of your competitors is an effective strategy in other industries as well. Two decades after emigrating from Taiwan, Janie and Victor Tsao wanted to pursue the American dream. Victor was 37 and Janie was 35 when they decided to start their own business. They were familiar with Taiwanese manufacturing companies, and they decided to start making computer products they could sell in the United States.

With two small children, Janie and Victor wanted to avoid taking on debt or bringing in investors, so they decided to hedge their bet. Both had a background in information technology, Janie at Carter Hawley Hale and Victor at Taco Bell. Because Victor was making a little more money, he kept his job while Janie quit in 1988 to work full time on their fledgling start-up. By 1991, they were generating enough income that Victor quit his job and took over as CEO, while Janie traveled the country drumming up business as vice president of business development.

With a technology background in networks and information systems and a lifelong familiarity with manufacturers in Taiwan, the Tsaos decided to make network products. As two hopeful entrepreneurs funding a tiny start-up from savings, they didn't want to take on Cisco in the business market, knowing it was a battle they could never win. Instead, they avoided Cisco completely, focusing their efforts entirely on the home networking market.

At the time, home networking was such a small niche that it barely existed. Their first product, a device called MultiShare, let several computers share a printer. As the company grew slowly and steadily, Janie and Victor reinvested their earnings and gradually carved out a niche in the market. By 1994, after six years in business, Victor finally started taking a salary. Sales at the time were $6.5 million, and the company had 55 employees. Linksys products were primarily sold through high-tech catalogs such as *Black Box* and *PC Connection*.

Linksys got a lucky break in 1995 when Microsoft introduced Windows 95. Prior to that, anyone using Linksys products had to install and configure software in order to network computers together. Windows 95 included built-in networking functions, making it simple to set up a network at home. At the same time, Janie's tenacious efforts placed Linksys products with several retailers. Janie and Victor continued adding new products, using off-the-shelf technology, but focused on making the products simple and easy to use. Sales soared, hitting $21.5 million in 1996 and $32.1 million in 1997.[8]

As the home broadband market developed, Linksys's portfolio of home networking products expanded, firmly establishing it as a contender in home routers, switches, and hubs. As more people started using cable and DSL modems at home, Linksys was perfectly positioned to grow with the market. After more than a decade of making products for home users, they had the experience, distribution agreements, and manufacturing savvy to pull it off.

The turning point for the company came in 2000. For years, pundits had predicted the explosion in broadband. Several companies rode the boom on high expectations, only to crash when those predictions didn't come true. As the market developed, retailers suggested Linksys build a broadband router so people using DSL or a cable modem could let several computers share one Internet connection.[9]

At the time, Cisco dominated the market for routers, but its cheapest version was $500, much too expensive and complicated for a home office customer.

Keeping his focus on the home market, Victor worked with his manufacturing partners in Taiwan to develop an easy-to-use, four-port router for the home office. Unlike the complicated and expensive business routers, the Linksys router used a simple browser program to walk customers through the installation. Best of all, he priced it at $199. It was the first router sold for less than $300, and sales exploded. Linksys revenue went from $107.6 million to $206.5 million.[10]

Another Linksys success story grew out of a near disaster. Repeating its strategy of bypassing the competition, Linksys began selling broadband routers in Canada while most of its competitors avoided doing so because of hardware compatibility fears. Seeing an opportunity, Victor jumped in with both feet. After shipping its first batch of routers north and getting a deluge of customer complaints, the company learned that its devices weren't compatible with Rogers, the Canadian telecommunications company.

Victor quickly dispatched several technicians to Canada. They rented a motel room in Niagara Falls and ordered a DSL line directly into their motel room.[11] Then they worked around the clock to solve the problem. Although it took several weeks, they eventually found the problem and corrected it. By expanding to a market where its competitors had no presence, Linksys bypassed them completely. This near miss also had another benefit: Linksys was seen as the only company that could make its system work in Canada.[12] By steering around its competitors and tackling a problem others avoided, Linksys established a strong foothold in a lucrative market, as well as a boost to its reputation.

In 15 years, Janie and Victor built their "mom-and-pop" company into a home networking powerhouse. Their decision to avoid competing with Cisco in the business market and focus on the home networking market eventually led to an interesting twist. When Cisco decided to expand into the home networking market in 2003, it bought Linksys for $500 million. In the beginning, Janie and Victor avoided Cisco as a matter of survival. In the long run, their strategy made Linksys even more valuable to the very competitor they wanted to avoid.

Bark Up a Different Tree

Bypassing the opposition isn't a strategy limited to start-ups. Even established industry players can effectively use this approach instead of running into a tough competitor like a brick wall. When Procter & Gamble (P&G) bought premium pet-food maker Iams in 1999, it was a huge blow to PETCO and PETsMART. Until then, the two pet superstores had the premium dog food market to themselves. P&G decided to increase sales by selling Iams pet food in grocery stores and other mass outlets for the first time.[13] With the premium pet food no longer available to lure shoppers, PETCO and PETsMART were in serious trouble. Even more ominous was the news that Wal-Mart would be selling Iams. As in many other categories, Wal-Mart was already the biggest seller of pet food in the United States through its Old Roy brand of dog food.

The pet stores soon discovered the bad news was even worse than it first appeared. In addition to taking away a key piece of their revenue in pet food, the change had a trickle-down effect in other areas. When customers went to the pet store to buy pet food, they usually wound up buying other pet-related products as well. When they didn't come in for pet food, they didn't make those impulse purchases, and the impact on sales was far greater. As PETsMART CEO Phil Francis pointed out, "Then there was the bone that wasn't bought because the customer wasn't there buying food."[14]

To combat the move by Wal-Mart into their terrain, the two pet superstores adopted different strategies. PETsMART initially decided to stand and fight, adopting a broad "everyday low-price" strategy that put it directly in Wal-Mart's line of fire. PETCO CEO Brian Devine took a different approach, electing to bypass this new competition in its core business, much the same as Trader Joe's did in avoiding direct competition with 7-Eleven.

Instead of trying to compete with Wal-Mart on price, a highly risky proposition at best, PETCO repositioned itself as the pet store equivalent of Whole Foods Market,[15] focusing on high-end luxury pet products that wouldn't appeal to Wal-Mart's demographics and services that wouldn't fit Wal-Mart's model. By employing a "hit 'em where they ain't" strategy, PETCO conceded some of the low ground on pet food, while it made a concerted effort to do things that Wal-Mart couldn't.

While Wal-Mart can sell Old Roy and Iams dog food, it can't offer pet grooming, veterinary services, or obedience training classes. Even if Wal-Mart wanted to, health laws would prohibit it from having animals in the same place they're selling food and groceries. PETCO went into high gear in all three areas. PETCO also began stocking more expensive luxury merchandise ranging from puppy pajamas and igloo doghouses to automatic pet drinking fountains and hundreds of pet toys. PETCO stores also added a grooming salon, pet training classes, and pet adoption centers. After all, when you adopt a pet, you buy pet supplies. Many stores also added rows of aquariums with tropical fish, along with all the assorted aquarium supplies. All these additions are things that don't make sense for Wal-Mart.

PETsMART quickly recognized the wisdom of this strategy and followed suit, making its own push into high-end merchandise and services. Taking a page of Wal-Mart's own playbook, PETsMART launched a program called "Customer Service Unleashed," with employees greeting customers at the door and answering their pet-care questions. At the same time, the company remodeled many existing stores, putting the grooming and veterinary centers front and center. "We used to treat services as a Third World country," said Robert F. Moran, president of PETsMART's North American stores. "Now it's more about service than product."[16]

PETsMART took services one step further, opening full-service veterinary clinics in its stores in partnership with Banfield Animal Hospital. "It works out really well for both of us," said Christine Mumford, director of the Banfield Animal Hospital in St. Louis, which is located inside PETsMART. "People come in for appointments and we take them through the store to pick up other things."[17]

With their new strategies in place, both pet superstores were soon out of danger and back on solid ground. In each case, competition from Wal-Mart no longer looked life threatening. On the contrary, both were profitable and growing, and both saw their margins *improve* after they lost exclusivity on Iams pet food.[18]

In the two years after it lost exclusivity on its most profitable product, PETCO racked up eight consecutive quarters of more than 30 percent growth in services income. Sales per square foot increased from $157 to $188, and gross margin increased from 25.6 percent to 31.2 percent.[19]

During the same period, PETsMART's margins increased from 23.8 percent to 29.2 percent, and earnings per share went from a $0.28 loss to a $0.69 profit.[20] By focusing on upscale products and adding unique services to avoid direct competition with Wal-Mart, both companies actually *improved* their margins and increased their profits.

Don't Fight Them on Their Own Turf

In addition to bypassing competitors strategically, you can also go around them geographically. When he launched easyJet in 1995, Stelios Haji-Ioannou decided to fly out of Luton Airport, which is about 50 kilometers north of London. Although Heathrow or Gatwick are more convenient for travelers, both are effectively controlled by British Airways, and are much more expensive. Luton is farther out of the way, but Stelios knew the lower cost would translate into significant savings for his customers. He also knew it would be difficult to make his business viable if he tried to fight the larger airlines on their own turf.

To convince customers it was worth the inconvenience to fly out of Luton, Stelios promoted easyJet's £29 one-way fares to Glasgow with an ad that said, "Fly to Scotland for the price of a pair of jeans." Critics thought both the ads and the airline were way off base, predicting that nobody would fly from Luton.[21] They were dead wrong. His low fares that drastically undercut British Airways proved irresistible even to business travelers, and easyJet leaped off the runway.

David Neeleman used the same strategy when he launched JetBlue, flying into California via Long Beach instead of LAX, and Oakland instead of SFO. Before JetBlue signed a gate agreement in Long Beach, the airport was just another second-tier airport. Other airlines wanted to fly out of LAX so they could use it as a hub for connecting flights. David Neeleman didn't agree. Like Stelios, he knew that keeping costs down was more important, and by avoiding direct competition in LAX, he had a competitive advantage.

After JetBlue started operating out of Long Beach, effectively establishing a low-cost beachhead in the Los Angeles market, American Airlines suddenly decided that it really needed to operate more flights out of Long Beach. American petitioned the Long Beach City Council, and ultimately won a token victory when the city reassigned five of

JetBlue's 27 landing slots: three to American and two to Alaska Air.[22] Even with a handful of gates in Long Beach, American has a much higher cost structure than JetBlue, and it continued bleeding red ink while JetBlue was solidly profitable.

Although this strategy of bypassing competitors geographically isn't unique, it's often dismissed as impractical—even when it might not be. Consider the flip side. If Stelios had decided he *really* needed to fly out of Heathrow, or David Neeleman decided he *really* needed to fly out of LAX, how could either have been competitive? Each would have been just another small fish in a pond full of sharks, and neither would have been able to differentiate themselves from their competitors. By going to smaller airports and keeping their costs down, both were able to offer much lower fares and fly circles around their bigger competitors.

The same principle is true in other industries. For restaurants and retails stores, the age-old wisdom about the key to success is *location, location, location*. Yet both the Outback Steakhouse and Trader Joe's defy conventional wisdom, choosing locations away from prime retail areas in favor of less expensive sites that may be a little off the beaten path. Both companies have great reputations and loyal customers, so premium real estate isn't as important to them. By choosing less expensive locations, they keep operating costs down, serving up higher profits for the companies and better values for their customers.

Discretion Is the Better Part of Valor

When you're outgunned and outnumbered, avoidance is a smart strategy. By avoiding competition with 7-Eleven and later with supermarkets, Trader Joe's evolved and improved, creating a completely new retailing category. When PETCO and PETsMART faced an impending disaster, they avoided a bloody battle with Wal-Mart by focusing on higher margin products and adding unique services, while in the process increasing profits for both companies. The near-disaster and increased competition turned out to be a blessing in disguise for both companies. Like Outback Steakhouse and Trader Joe's, easyJet and JetBlue flew in the face of conventional wisdom by selecting less expensive locations to keep their costs down. Like the smart kid walking away from the school bully, it's better to pick the fights you can win and steer clear of the rest.

Chapter 3

Leverage the Idea,
Not Your Time

In most companies, your horizons are limited by your resources. In effect, your sales can only grow as fast as the money, time,
and people available to create those sales. In fact, fast-growing companies often run into major cash flow problems because they need more
and more cash to meet rapidly increasing demand. By stepping off the
traditional path and looking at it from a different angle, you'll realize
that's not necessarily true. What if you could get all your competitors to
promote and sell your brand? Or even make your product for you?
What if you could increase sales 1,000 percent without spending an
extra dollar buying materials or equipment, or an extra hour of labor
producing it? *That's* leveraging the idea.

The principle of leverage is simple. Just like it's easier to lift a car
using a jack, leveraging your strengths can help you extend your brand
and increase your sales *without* overextending your company. The most
widely used example of leverage is franchising. Instead of opening its
own stores, and using its own time, money, and resources, McDonald's
leveraged its strengths (store operations) by having thousands of people
around the globe open McDonald's stores. Ron Joyce did the same thing
with Tim Hortons, opening far more stores by franchising than he ever
could have opened on his own. The same principle holds true in other
industries. Looking for the leverage points can give you a competitive
advantage in areas where you least expect it.

Leverage in a Bottle

Jim Koch raised more than a few eyebrows when the Harvard MBA told his friends he was quitting his $250,000 a year consulting job to open his own brewery. In 1984, he launched the Boston Beer Company with $140,000 in savings, another $100,000 from friends, and a recipe handed down by his great-great-great-grandfather.[1] Jim raised even more eyebrows when he started brewing his signature Samuel Adams Boston Lager and announced a decision that flew in the face of conventional wisdom, and ultimately played a key role in the company's success.

Before Jim started the Boston Beer Company, there were really only two kinds of breweries in the United States—the large multinationals such as Anheuser-Busch and Coors, and the small microbreweries. The big companies produced millions of gallons of beer a year, with quality that was acceptable, but not the best. The microbreweries, on the other hand, were known for their artisan approach to brewing. They had great tasting premium beer, but they could only brew it in small batches. Furthermore, the quality was always a wild card. Most microbrewers were small operations working on limited budgets, so they started out with bad equipment and had quality control problems. As Jim explains, "Brewing requires operating room standards of sanitation and quality control. You can't do that in a bunch of tanks you got out of a dairy farm and a bottling line that was a used soda line."[2]

With Sam Adams, Jim wanted to create a microbrewery product with consistently high quality that he could produce on a much larger scale. Because quality was his primary concern, followed closely by growth, the logical conclusion would be to build a new brewery and invest heavily in state-of-the-art equipment. Instead, he came up with a different approach that gave him the high quality and growth potential he wanted, but with almost no investment in infrastructure. He decided not to brew his own beer.

Find the Leverage Points for Quality

The immediate reaction when people heard about Jim's strategy was almost always the same: *That will never work!* After all, how could he control the quality if someone else was brewing his beer? In fact, the exact opposite was true. By contracting out the brewing, Jim could spend much *more* of his time focusing on the quality of the beer. As a small start-up, contracting out the brewing also let him produce and sell much larger volumes of very high-quality beer than he ever could have if he brewed it himself.

With the benefit of his heritage in beer and his experience in manufacturing, Jim had a pretty good idea what to look for in a partner to do his brewing. He discussed it with his father and they came up with a list of breweries that could make a 19th century recipe with modern quality control. Then he called breweries with an unusual proposal: he would bring the recipe and ingredients, and they would do the brewing. Although it was an unusual idea, Pittsburgh Brewing Company was excited by it. The company wasn't brewing five days a week, so it had spare capacity. They quickly struck a deal, and Sam Adams had a home.

Jim's strategy was to find the leverage points for quality and concentrate on them. The fact that he didn't have to worry about buying and maintaining his own equipment let him focus on the things that did affect quality in Samuel Adams beer. Physical ownership of the equipment is not one of them. "The leverage points are the recipe, the ingredients, and the care and attention that go into the brewing of it," Jim said. For example, Boston Beer Company is the only brewer of any significant size in the world where the owner and the brewer personally select every lot of hops. Since the beginning, Jim has traveled to Europe every year with his brewmasters, going through hundreds of farmers' batches of hops to pick the best ones. As he's discovered, there are quality differences every year on every farm. Personally buying only the best quality ingredients is one way to ensure quality.

When it comes to quality in the actual brewing process, where Sam Adams might seem to be most vulnerable under a contracting agreement, Jim has an obvious answer. "If they don't do it right, I can leave," he said. "We are a very significant piece of their production, so at the ownership level, if we leave, the brewery may not be viable. At the plant worker level, they know that if they screw up and I leave, they lose their job."

Even so, he doesn't leave it up to chance. Jim's unique arrangement frees his eight full-time brewmasters from many of the routine operational issues that have nothing to do with the quality of the beer. In addition to overseeing the actual production of the beer, the typical brewmaster has to supervise equipment maintenance, fill out manning charts and schedules, order supplies, schedule production lines, manage the labor force, and make sure there are tanks open downstream to take the beer they're about to produce. While those day-to-day details are necessary to run a brewery, they're not related to the quality of the beer. "Our brewmasters don't have to do any of that," Jim points out. "Their whole job is to make sure we have a river of perfect Samuel Adams flowing from the brewery to the customer."[3]

Boston Beer Company grew 40 percent a year as Samuel Adams built a loyal following, and it eventually became the mainstay of Pittsburgh Brewing Company's output. Jim later made similar agreements with breweries in Oregon, Washington, and New York, giving him geographic distribution as well.[4]

In an interesting twist, several years after Sam Adams was an established brand and resources were no longer an issue, Jim eventually bought his own brewery in Cincinnati. He didn't buy it until well *after* Boston Beer Company was big enough to deal with all the day-to-day management operations in running a brewery. Today, Boston Beer Company brews about half of the beer itself and contracts out the other half. Contracting out the brewing at the outset was a key factor in the company's success—both in maintaining the quality and in producing higher volumes to make Samuel Adams a national brand.

"The microbreweries that came and went before Sam Adams did not have a consistent level of quality, so nobody could drink them very long before they ran into an infected beer," Jim said. "We had consistently high-quality beer, which allowed a lot of people to become brand loyal. You could be a Sam Adams drinker and always get a great beer."

By combining an 18th century recipe and a 21st century idea, Jim built Sam Adams into an award-winning brand with a loyal following. Boston Beer Company now brews 1.2 million barrels of Samuel Adams beer every year, producing $250 million in revenues.[5] Jim could not have done that by following the traditional formula. "You find the leverage points for quality," Jim explains. "Ownership of physical assets might be. In this case, it's not. So you just figure out where you've got leverage."

From Doughnuts to Dollars

Most people who own doughnut shops consider bakeries, coffee shops, and grocery stores that sell doughnuts as competitors. Not Krispy Kreme. Despite the fact that Krispy Kreme spends an incredible amount of money building its own stores (twice as much as Dunkin' Donuts), the company bends over backwards to foster relationships with would-be competitors, turning them into "off-premises partners." Krispy Kreme used this unconventional approach to build a thriving "off-premises partner" program to supply doughnuts to its competitors.

Each Krispy Kreme store features a live factory tour, where visitors can watch doughnuts being made, which is part of its overall goal of creating a captivating experience. Watching the dough going in one end of the machine and freshly baked doughnuts coming out the other is an impressive sight. Creating this "doughnut theater" isn't cheap—the doughnut maker alone costs $350,000, and with all the other costs associated with building and operating a store, it can cost up to $1.4 million for each location.[6]

With that kind of investment, you would think both the company and the franchisee would be fiercely protective of their store locations. It might come as a surprise to learn that every Krispy Kreme location has a thriving wholesale business, selling doughnuts "off premises" to supermarkets, bakeries, convenience stores, and even college campuses. At first glance, this strategy doesn't seem to make sense. After all, if you can buy Krispy Kreme doughnuts at the grocery store, why bother to visit the Krispy Kreme outlet that cost so much to build?

If you consider idle capacity, you'll see why Krispy Kreme's indirect strategy makes so much sense. If an airline seat or a hotel room is empty, the company will never get that money back. The same is true for Krispy Kreme. Each Krispy Kreme store can make between 50,000 and 120,000 doughnuts a day—far more than it can sell from its retail counters or drive-through windows.[7] If a store is capable of producing 50,000 doughnuts a day but is only selling 10,000, that's 40,000 in "lost" sales.

"During non-peak hours we have excess capacity, so we're just like any manufacturer at that point. Idle capacity becomes a cost," CEO Scott Livengood explains. Using those idle times to make and ship doughnuts to off-premise partners actually increases sales, rather than cannibalizing them.[8] Instead of jealously guarding its product, Krispy Kreme leverages the opportunity by recruiting other partners to sell its product.

While some diehards might still insist that selling through supermarkets and convenience stores hurts in-store sales, consider the numbers. The average Krispy Kreme location does almost $3 million in sales a year. Despite the fact that it only had 276 stores nationwide by 2003, Krispy Kreme had 24 percent market share of packaged doughnut sales in grocery and convenience stores nationwide.[9]

Krispy Kreme produces about 2 billion doughnuts annually in its 276 stores.[10] Dunkin' Donuts, which has 3,600 stores in the United States alone, makes about 2.1 billion doughnuts a year. As Dunkin' Donuts franchisees are quick to point out, that's not a fair comparison because they don't sell to off-site partners. And that's exactly the point. By taking a broader view of partners and competitors, Krispy Kreme successfully leveraged its investment and extended its brand.

Coming Up Shorts

A year after Jim Koch started brewing Samuel Adams, 27-year-old Nicholas (Nick) Graham moved from Calgary, Alberta, to San Francisco. His punk rock career wasn't supporting him, and he didn't have enough money to buy the skinny ties that were in fashion at the time, so he started making his own to sell to shops around town. He called on a buyer from Macy's West to show his ties, including some with unusual, offbeat patterns. Madonna was beginning to popularize men's underwear at the time, and young people were starting to wear boxer shorts outside their clothing. The Macy's buyer said the print from one of Nick's ties would make great boxer shorts. He mocked up a couple pairs of boxers at her suggestion and a new company was born.[11]

From the outset, Nick started a different kind of company. He came up with wacky, off-beat ideas that became his signature, such as the Imperial Hoser, a red tartan boxer with a detachable raccoon tail. He named his company JOE BOXER and appointed himself "chief underpants officer."

During his first year in business, Nick decided to put pictures of $100 bills on boxer shorts, figuring they would sell. A neighbor's son found some of Nick's silk screens in the trash and showed them to his father, who immediately called the police. The next day, the Secret Service showed up to investigate a possible counterfeiting ring, and JOE BOXER accidentally became a media sensation. All the local papers and several news stations carried the story about the feds confiscating a thousand pairs of boxer shorts silk-screened with $100 bills and burning them in a bonfire.[12] Nick was amazed and delighted by all the free publicity he got. Without spending a penny on advertising, JOE BOXER was on its way to being a household name.

Part of JOE BOXER's appeal was the outrageousness itself. Customers were buying a fun, hip, slightly off-center brand that wasn't afraid to be tongue in cheek. JOE BOXER was the first to create glow-in-the-dark boxers, including one style that shows "No, No, No" when the lights are on and "Yes, Yes, Yes" when the lights are off. The biggest hit was Mr. Licky, a huge smiley face covering a pair of boxers with a tongue hanging out.

As the company grew, Nick continued his outrageous antics. In 1993, he sent 100 pairs of boxer shorts to President Clinton to commemorate his first 100 days in office. The note attached said, "If you're going to change the country, you've got to change your underwear." The next year, Nick and Virgin Airways CEO Richard Branson, famous for his equally outrageous publicity stunts, held the world's first in-flight underwear fashion show aboard a Virgin flight from London to San Francisco. With its notoriety increasing, the company moved beyond its roots of novelty boxer shorts, adding the JOE BOXER Girlfriend collection of sleepwear for women and the JOE BOXER Kids for children.

By its 10th anniversary, JOE BOXER had become a cultural icon. Madonna, the sizzling pop-icon who started the fashion trend, wore JOE BOXER pajamas in *Truth or Dare*. Quentin Tarantino wore them in *Pulp Fiction*. When Nick entered a race car in the Indianapolis 500, his motto was "No skid marks." Nick was even dressed as the queen of England when he was suspended over Times Square with his cohort Richard Branson to promote their new campaign—"Buy Five Pairs and Fly." The joint offer gave customers a free companion ticket on Virgin Airways if they bought five pairs of JOE BOXER underwear—a cheeky spin on easyJet's offer to "Fly to Scotland for the price of a pair of jeans."

By 2001, JOE BOXER was the number-one junior sleepwear brand in America, and it was also the fastest growing brand of white underwear. Nick Graham had done an amazing job of building a fun, cool, irreverent brand that was growing 25 percent a year—all without a traditional advertising budget. With a leader like Nick Graham, why spend money on ads?

Fraying at the Seams

Despite the company's phenomenal growth, JOE BOXER was starting to unravel. While Nick was out promoting JOE BOXER with his outrageous antics, he left the operational details to people he had hired. The company was manufacturing garments overseas under contract, and costs were getting out of control. By 2000, JOE BOXER had 150 employees and $100 million in revenue, but costs were rising as fast as sales. JOE BOXER had gone far beyond its traditional core market of novelty boxer shorts, and the complexity of the business increased dramatically as the company added new product lines. Despite ever-increasing sales, the company couldn't outrun its problems, and it racked up $13 million in debt. Nick brought in some investment bankers to try to sell the company, but in more than a year of talking to potential buyers, nobody came forward.

In 2001, the company made a fatal error. The new management team Nick brought in terminated a licensing agreement for women's undergarments, because it wanted to take that product line back in-house. The termination provisions weren't spelled out clearly in the contract, though, and the licensee promptly sued. The court sided with the licensee, agreeing that JOE BOXER had started manufacturing and selling products before the licensing agreement expired. In a devastating blow, the court awarded the licensee a $3 million judgment against JOE BOXER.

The company was already living on the edge financially, and was staggering under a significant debt load. There was no way it could pay the judgment. Nick continued looking for a corporate partner to find a way out, but nobody stepped forward. There were too many internal problems to fix and too much risk. Besides, if the company went bankrupt, a buyer might be able to pick up some of the assets much cheaper.

Saving JOE BOXER

Nick found a savior in Bill Sweedler, CEO of Windsong Allegiance, an apparel-licensing firm in Connecticut. Bill knew a thing or two about rolling with the punches and adapting to change. After learning the ropes at Polo Ralph Lauren, Bill went into business with his father, a veteran of the apparel industry, to create Windsong Allegiance in the early 1990s. Their original plan was to manufacture clothing in the Caribbean, taking advantage of lower costs and favorable trade relationships, and import it to the United States.

Working under contract to make clothing for companies such as Tommy Hilfiger, Windsong's plan was successful, but not very lucrative, and so it changed gears. Instead of contract manufacturing, Windsong began licensing other brands, producing products on its own and selling them to department stores. That strategy was more successful, but Bill realized that Windsong's biggest single expense was licensing fees. He was eager to get a brand of his own, and he kept his eyes and ears open. When he heard that investment bankers were shopping JOE BOXER around, Bill was interested.

When he arrived in San Francisco on a Friday afternoon to talk to Nick, JOE BOXER had already prepared a news release to announce its pending bankruptcy filing. Bill suggested they wait until Monday so they could discuss alternatives. Although the company was clearly on the ropes, Bill saw opportunity where bigger competitors saw trouble. He knew the JOE BOXER brand resonated with people, and he thought he could solve the operation problems. He was hungry to take over an established brand, and none was more exciting to him than the ultra hip, irreverent, sometimes wacky JOE BOXER.

Bill took a leap where the giants feared to tread, buying JOE BOXER and taking over as CEO. Having watched as major brands such as Martha Stewart Everday and Mossimo signed groundbreaking licensing agreements with Kmart and Target, he knew there was an opportunity to follow suit.[13] One of the first things Bill did after taking over was to call Kmart to discuss a licensing agreement.

At the time, Kmart stock was at a five-year high, and Martha Stewart had just renewed her exclusive deal with them. Bill knew that a mega-licensing deal with Kmart, Target, or Wal-Mart could extend the brand faster and further than selling through department stores. He proposed a licensing agreement for a new brand called "Republic of Joe" that would be exclusive to Kmart. Kmart wanted exclusivity on the JOE BOXER brand, and Bill said, "No way." It was a short conversation.

Two days later, Kmart called back and asked, "How much do you want?" That's a question that makes an entrepreneur's heart beat fast. The discussions went into high gear, and they quickly reached an agreement.

Under the traditional manufacturing model, Bill would have approached department stores and retail chains one by one, trying to convince each of them to carry JOE BOXER products. On the flip side, he'd have to be ready to ramp up production, finance the inventory, manufacture the products, drop ship merchandise to different retailers, and handle a thousand and one operational details—all the things that got JOE BOXER in trouble in the first place.

Instead, Bill followed the path blazed by Martha Stewart and Mossimo, signing a groundbreaking agreement with Kmart less than four months after taking over. Kmart would have an exclusive on the JOE BOXER brand, giving it prominent placement in every store. The agreement was a win for each side. JOE BOXER would benefit from the vastly increased distribution, landing in 2,100 Kmart stores and getting exposed to more than 130 million customers a year.[14] Kmart was also responsible for all advertising and promotions, eliminating another big expense.

If it was a great deal for JOE BOXER, it was an even a better deal for Kmart. After years of declining sales, the retailer's image was tarnished and the agreement represented far more than just adding another new brand. Kmart desperately wanted a strong brand that would appeal to younger shoppers, and JOE BOXER had brand recognition of 87 percent for customers between the ages of 12 and 34. Teenagers had no interest in Martha Stewart, but they loved JOE BOXER. It was a major coup, and they hoped JOE BOXER could bring some fun and excitement into Kmart, in addition to attracting a younger audience that hadn't been shopping at Kmart.[15]

Extend Your Brand—
Don't Overextend Your Company

In addition to getting JOE BOXER products in 2,100 stores virtually overnight, Bill took the leverage concept one step further. Under the agreement, Kmart—not JOE BOXER—would be responsible for all manufacturing. In one stroke of the pen, Bill eliminated a huge amount of the operating costs of the company. JOE BOXER no longer had to buy raw materials, manufacture products, or pay to ship them. The new business model completely changed the dynamics of the company, and Bill's risky acquisition looked more like a stroke of genius.

Freed from all the operational problems, Bill's team could focus on planning new products and carefully managing the brand. The only other thing they had to do was cash the check. Under the new business model, JOE BOXER has far more sales with far fewer operating costs. Today, the entire team at JOE BOXER is 15 people, compared to the 150 employees before the company got in trouble.[16]

When Kmart introduced JOE BOXER, it was the most successful product launch in Kmart history. According to Kmart CEO Jim Adamson, JOE BOXER not only exceeded sales expectations, but smashed them completely—all without advertising. To announce the Kmart launch, Nick Graham (still JOE BOXER's head cheerleader) led the launch party at Kmart's Astor Place store in New York City, complete with a marching band in boxer shorts and synchronized shopping carts.[17]

Without knowing it at the time, Bill's plan to leverage the JOE BOXER brand also avoided a potential catastrophe later. When he negotiated the licensing deal, Kmart was seemingly on solid ground financially. The stock was at a five-year high, and his investment bankers advised him that the company's credit rating was good. Nine months later, Kmart was bankrupt. If Bill had used a traditional supplier agreement, JOE BOXER could easily have been on the hook for millions in unpaid inventory. Instead, all the inventory was manufactured and already owned by Kmart, which virtually eliminated the potential risk for JOE BOXER.

By taking an established brand that had gotten into trouble and leveraging its core strengths, Bill rescued JOE BOXER and moved it in a completely new direction. In retrospect, his risky acquisition of a troubled company looks more like a brilliant strategic move from a creative thinker. As Bill said, "In our business, if you play it too safe, you're not going to be around too long."

Find the Leverage Points

Before Jim Koch came along, everybody knew that you couldn't control the quality in brewing beer unless you did it all yourself. And everybody was wrong. Jim Koch built Boston Beer Company into a $200 million business and Samuel Adams into a respected brand by focusing on the leverage points for quality, instead of trying to do everything himself. Bill Sweedler had a vision for JOE BOXER that was much bigger than anyone else imagined. He intuitively understood the magic of the brand, but he also understood the company's limitations. JOE BOXER was all about being fun, friendly, and outrageous. Manufacturing efficiency was never a core competence, and it likely never would be. By stepping outside the traditional boundaries, he created a corporate structure that greatly expanded JOE BOXER sales while decreasing the amount of complexity necessary to manage it. In each case, someone else handled the routine operations necessary to make their products, freeing up Jim Koch and Bill Sweedler to spend their time doing what they do well: managing their brands.

Krispy Kreme sells doughnuts through bakeries, supermarkets, and convenience stores that compete with its company-owned stores. In fact, the company goes to great lengths to encourage competition. Just like the Pittsburgh Brewing Company, Krispy Kreme would otherwise have idle capacity going to waste. Selling through off-premises partners lets it recapture that wasted capacity, and everybody wins. If you want to take a big idea and make it *really* big, look for the leverage points that will let you extend your brand without overextending your company.

Chapter 4

Shamelessly Copy Good Ideas

When Fred Smith launched FedEx using a central hub to ship packages around the country, it seemed like a novel idea. Instead of shipping a package from New York to Boston, it was routed through Memphis, loaded onto a different plane, and sent out again from there. While that method may sound inefficient for one transaction, it's tremendously efficient when you put all the transactions on a network together. Although it was a revolutionary idea when it came to shipping packages, the idea wasn't really new at all. It's the same concept used to switch calls through a telecommunications switch or a clearinghouse. As Fred explained, "I certainly didn't invent the concept. The post office in India used it. Delta Airlines used it. But applying it to the world of logistics was unique."[1]

Copying a successful idea is as old as the Nile. When somebody comes up with an idea to give them a competitive advantage, it won't be long before everyone else copies it. That's not to say you should infringe on another company's intellectual property. Of course not. But there's nothing wrong with copying good ideas. Like Fred Smith, you can find some of the best ideas by looking outside your industry for ideas that you can apply to your business. The reality is that emulating good ideas makes sense. If somebody has figured out a better way to do something, why not learn from it?

Follow the Leaders

Gary Hoover first started thinking about opening his own retail store when he was a retail analyst on Wall Street. Like any good analyst, he started by doing his homework, trying to identify what the hot new concept would be for the next 20 years (the 1980s and 90s). He realized the superstore concept was a breakthrough in retailing, and the more he learned about it, the more convinced he became that this would be the next big thing.

Charles Lazarus introduced the superstore concept, opening the first Toys "R" Us superstore in Washington, D.C. His idea was to get customers out of the mall and into strip centers, where they could park close to the door. By offering a huge selection at discount prices, he created a phenomenon that ultimately became the largest player in the toy industry. Watching as Toys "R" Us grew, Gary continued to study the company. As a public company, its numbers were readily available and he could understand the Toys "R" Us model.

Gary continued kicking the idea around while he worked for other retailers, first as a buyer for Federated Department Stores and later as vice president of marketing, planning, and research for May Department Stores. Although the superstore concept was still limited to toys at the time, he was convinced it would sweep through other areas of retail. He also looked at the aging population, which was a key factor underlining the whole economy, and came up with a list of areas in retail where he thought superstores would be successful: auto parts, home improvement, books, records, toys, and sporting goods.

He researched and studied the opportunities for seven years. It was pretty obvious to Gary that superstores could, and would, be created in all those areas. He just had to pick one. He wasn't the type to work on his own car or fix up his house, but he loved to read and hang out in bookstores. A book superstore seemed like a perfect fit for him.

When he finally decided he'd better act on his idea or give it up, Gary did one last round of homework. He attended a bookseller's convention, and what he heard shocked him at first. Then it encouraged him. Speaker after speaker had a negative vision of the industry, citing statistics that people weren't reading as much anymore and illiteracy was on the rise. The consensus seemed to be that there was no future in books.

"I just couldn't believe they were pessimistic about the future of the industry, which I thought was pretty exciting," Gary said. Even more surprising was that nobody was talking about superstores. When he attended the workshops about the future of the bookstore and not one person mentioned the superstore concept, he was convinced he had a winner. "I don't know if any of them had ever been in a Toys "R" Us store or read one of their annual reports," Gary said. "I realized they weren't doing the same research I was." With that, he made his decision and launched a new venture.

As a veteran in retailing, but a newcomer to selling books, Gary approached venture capitalists to raise $3 million to open a book superstore in Chicago. They laughed at the idea. He then scaled down his plans, realizing he wouldn't bring in enough money to pursue his dream right away, and he brought in $350,000 from angel investors.

Ever the analyst, he also took an analytical approach to opening his first store. "I had to find a city where the ratio of demand for books to the cost of operating a bookstore was the highest."[2] In essence, he wanted to find a location where he could get the most bang for the buck—high demand and low operating cost. Big metropolitan areas such as New York and Chicago were off the list because of the high cost of operating in a large metro area. Instead, he identified four college towns: Ann Arbor, Madison, Research Triangle Park, and Austin. He settled on Austin, then packed up and moved there in 1982.

Take a Page out of Their Book

Having taken the plunge, Gary took what he believed was the essence of Toys "R" Us stores—a huge selection and discount prices—and applied it to books. At the time, the biggest bookstores were B. Dalton Bookseller and Waldenbooks, both of which operated hundreds of small stores in malls. Gary's first Bookstop store was 10,000 square feet, almost unheard of for a bookstore at the time. He also took the unprecedented approach of selling books at a discount every day. Toys "R" Us was also particularly adept at using distribution centers, which nobody in the book industry was using at the time. Instead, the major chains such as B. Dalton and Waldenbooks had inventory drop shipped to each store. As Bookstop grew, Gary built distribution centers in Florida, Texas, and California to serve three parts of the nation.

In addition to learning lessons from Toys "R" Us, Gary emulated good ideas he saw in other industries. While a typical bookstore layout had one main aisle down the middle, he borrowed the raceway design from supermarkets. Bookstop stores had an oval path near the outside of the store, with best-sellers in the back, children's books on one side, and periodicals on the other, so the book placement would "drive" people all the way around the store. He also like the way Radio Shack captured customers' names and addresses so it could market to them later. He didn't want to bother customers when they were in his store, though, so he came up with a new twist: he offered customers a discount card good for 10 percent off any additional purchases if they signed up. In addition to getting their names and addresses, Bookstop also got to see what they were buying and how often. In the process, he introduced the first loyalty card in the book industry.

By taking good ideas in different industries and applying them to bookselling, Gary built Bookstop into the fourth largest book retailer in the nation. In 1989, Barnes & Noble bought the company, and Bookstop became a cornerstone of Barnes & Noble Superstores. Even though he was a newcomer to the book industry, Gary learned from others before him in different industries and applied their successful formulas to selling books. By applying the example of Charles Lazarus and Toys "R" Us to the bookselling business, he helped redefine the industry.

Good Ideas Will Always Fly

When Gordon Bethune took over Continental Airlines, the company seemed headed for its third trip to bankruptcy. After 10 years of cost cutting, a series of management teams had cut pay, eliminated jobs, alienated customers, and effectively wiped out morale at the company. At the time, Continental was ranked dead last in on-time performance, and the company was spending more than $5 million a month rebooking passengers on other airlines because its flights had arrived too late to make connections. When he took over as CEO, Gordon Bethune knew he would have to do something to earn the trust of Continental employees. He also had to stop the bleeding—fast!

As part of his "Go Forward" plan to save the company, Gordon announced that he would pay every employee $65 each time Continental placed among the top five airlines in the Transportation Department's monthly on-time performance rating. This was a clear-cut objective, and because it was measured by an outside organization, it was completely impartial. If the company ranked in the top five, every single employee, regardless of position, got the bonus. In a company that was suspicious of management, Gordon figured it was a simple, impartial objective that could get everyone pulling in the same direction. Equally important, it could help restore a sense of pride and teamwork among Continental's employees.

Within one month, Continental moved from last place to fourth in on-time performance. Every employee got the bonus. Instead of just adding it to their paychecks, employees received an extra check for $65. For employees who had been on the wrong end of a bad relationship, this simple step was concrete evidence that change was in the air. The following month, Continental ranked first in on-time performance. The company paid out $2.5 million in bonuses, but the cost was more than offset by the $5 million it saved by arriving on time.[3]

After Continental began consistently ranking at the top in on-time performance, Gordon tweaked the program so they had to be in the top three to get the bonus, but he also increased the bonus to $100. The change was set to take place the following January, but when Continental was number one in on-time performance in December, he paid each employee $100 anyway—even though the new bonus hadn't taken effect.[4] Employees were delighted, and the excited buzz in the hallways increased as they realized that for the first time in recent memory, the senior executives actually seemed to care about them.

Although there were many other factors in his turnaround of Continental, the on-time bonus was a clear, measurable signal to employees that they could make a difference if they worked together as a team. "65 bucks was a nice way of saying thank you to a bunch of people who learned that the only way to get the 65 bucks is when they all work together," Gordon said. "And it's been working for us ever since. It's not a lot, but it doesn't sometimes take a lot to show that this is like an appreciative change in the way we behave."[5]

Like a head coach recognizing a great play from an opposing team, others in the industry copied Gordon's idea. When Jeff McClelland took over as president and chief operating officer at America West in

1999, the company was hitting a lot of turbulence. Customer service was poor, morale was low, and it had just been fined by the Federal Aviation Administration for lax maintenance. Taking a page from Continental's playbook, Jeff convinced his new boss, CEO Doug Parker, to offer a $50 bonus to all America West employees anytime they ranked in the top three in on-time performance.

In one slight twist, they expanded the program, awarding the $50 bonus anytime the airline was ranked in the top three in either on-time performance or fewest customer complaints. Before long, America West had gone from the bottom of the list to consistently ranking near the top. Not surprisingly, morale improved significantly and the company turned around. "When I came here, people didn't like saying they worked for America West. They didn't feel like they had support of senior management," said Jeff, a former Navy pilot and Stanford MBA. "Today people actually like working for America West."[6]

Ask for Advice

Learning from other people's success doesn't have to be on the sly. After getting his new magazine *Negro Digest* off the ground in 1942, John Johnson quickly realized he was in over his head. Never having published a magazine before, he didn't know the inner workings of the publishing industry. Knowing what he didn't know, John approached Henry Luce, the publisher at Time-Life, to ask for advice.

When John finally got the meeting, he explained that he had just started a magazine and simply wanted advice. The Time-Life publisher called in editors and business managers from all parts of the company, and John talked to experts in the New York office and returned to Chicago for additional meetings with Time-Life circulation and promotion departments.[7]

Most entrepreneurs, and business leaders in general, fall into the trap of thinking they know it all, or thinking they're supposed to know it all. The biggest mistake you can make is not to ask for advice when you're on unfamiliar ground. Simply by asking for advice from others in his industry, John learned invaluable lessons, and likely avoided costly mistakes, in getting his new venture off the ground. These lessons and relationships helped him again later when he launched *Ebony* and *Jet* magazines, and John went on to build a publishing empire.

Krispy Kreme CEO Scott Livengood did the same thing before expanding the doughnut chain outside the Southeast. He knew expanding nationwide could be a tricky proposition, so he traveled around the country visiting restaurant owners and food service companies, asking what to expect and what problems they had run into. He spent three days in Oakbrook, Illinois, at the McDonald's headquarters, and talked with 20 of its department heads. "They were willing to share their best practices with me," Scott said. "I've personally met with every CEO of every major food concept chain to learn from the things they were doing well."[8] Learning from other companies was time well spent, and he grew Krispy Kreme from a small base in the Southeast to more than 300 locations nationwide in the next three years. *Restaurants & Institutions* magazine later named Scott "Executive of the Year" after he led the most successful IPO of the year in a down market.[9]

Asking for advice doesn't have to be confined to those in your own line of business. You can learn a lot by visiting similar companies with which you don't directly compete. When Lawrence "Larry" Perlman took over Control Data's disk drive business in the mid-1980s, it was bleeding badly. Under pressure from Japanese competitors who were producing higher quality drives at lower costs, Control Data was losing money on every drive it produced.

To learn how to improve the manufacturing process, Larry spent a lot of time in Tokyo at the Toyota and Seiko plants learning Japanese business practices. He even flew rank and file workers and front line managers to Japan for a week so they could see firsthand how Japanese companies operated. Control Data copied the playbook from Toyota and Seiko, cutting out layers of middle management, focusing on teams, and giving them autonomy to make decisions on the shop floor. In the process, Larry turned Control Data's disk drive business around and later sold it to Seagate.[10]

Look Outside Your Industry

In the mid-1980s, when Target was getting poor marks on customer service and disappointing customers, George Jones, Target's executive vice president for store operations, recognized the problem and made a commitment to invest in customer service. After months of studying cultures at various companies, George adopted the Walt Disney Company's customer service program. Emulating the Disney program, customers were called "guests" and employees "team members," and the company launched "Target University" with training and coursework on understanding customer motivation and projecting an enthusiastic attitude.[11]

Like Disney theme parks, Target put more workers on the floor to assist shoppers. Target also relaxed the strict rules that made it difficult to solve customer problems, which allowed team members to use common sense when a problem arose. George also realized that store visits by senior executives had become a command performance that intimidated employees and stifled feedback. Instead, visits began to take place informally without advance notice. Target even changed its mission statement from a "self-service" to "assisted self-service" company to reflect the new direction. "He strongly believed in Disney's concepts and Disney's training program," former Target CEO Floyd Hall explained. "All good ideas are meant to be stolen, and Disney was considered then—and now—one of the best at customer service."[12]

When General Mills was looking for ways to improve its supply chain operation, Randy Darcy, senior vice president of supply chain operations, turned to NASCAR for ideas. The maker of Cheerios, Wheaties, Yoplait Yogurt, and Betty Crocker meals was taking up to four and a half hours to change production lines from one type of food to another. What better source for information on quick changeovers than a Winston Cup pit crew? One thing the General Mills team learned from the pit crew was to videotape the changeover, then have the whole team critique it to look for ways to improve. In the process, they cut the changeover time from four and a half hours down to 12 minutes. Once the new timesaving ideas were tested in one location, they were implemented throughout the company. According to Randy Darcy, the ideas from NASCAR saved General Mills millions of dollars.[13]

Randy continued looking for new ideas in unusual places, sending a group to train with the U.S. marshal's SWAT team to learn about teamwork. Based on that experience, General Mills changed bonuses to cover the entire supply chain. With different goals for each department, purchasing might have bought thinner cardboard because it cost less, even if the lighter box was more difficult to use in manufacturing because it was less stable. Under the new system, nobody could reach his or her objectives unless everybody did.[14]

Learn From the Best

You can't copyright good ideas. When you see something working, whether it's in the same industry or not, consider what impact it would have in your organization. Doug Hoover built Bookstop into the first book superstore chain by copying business and distribution ideas from Toys "R" Us, and the raceway around the store from supermarkets. He also borrowed an idea from Radio Shack to create the first loyalty card. By studying other companies, he found ideas that worked and applied them to the bookselling business.

John Johnson turned to veteran magazine publishers for advice, and built Johnson Publishing into a media empire. Target turned to Disney, and General Mills turned to NASCAR to get ideas to improve their companies. You don't have to have all the answers, and you certainly don't need to constantly come up with original ideas. Finding out what works in other companies and applying it to your business lets you learn from their experience. As the old saying goes, the early bird may get the worm, but the second mouse gets the cheese.

Chapter 5

Put All Your Eggs in One Basket

Diversification can be a good thing, but it can also be dangerous. When you see car companies buying banks, soft drink companies buying restaurants, and tobacco companies buying anybody, it can stretch the limits of imagination for even the strongest proponents of synergy. When venturing into unfamiliar terrain, don't expect automatic success. That's not to say you should try to be a one-trick pony, but sticking to your roots can often be a very profitable strategy.

At first glance, it may not seem like a hamburger joint, an Internet search engine, and a software company have much in common. In fact, In-N-Out Burger, Google, and Borland have all succeeded by sticking to the same strategy: focusing on one thing, and doing that one thing extremely well. Instead of trying to be all things to all people, all three companies have succeeded by keeping a tight strategic focus in one core area that is executed extremely well. As Mark Twain said, "Put all your eggs in one basket—and watch that basket!"

Create Your Own Cult

When Harry and Esther Snyder opened their first hamburger stand in 1948, there were no seats, and unlike many other burger stands at the time, no car hops. Instead, they attached a two-way speaker box and opened what many believe is California's first drive-thru hamburger stand. In-N-Out put quality over growth, sticking to the same basic formula from the outset. Harry and Esther opened the second In-N-Out three years later, and they reinvested their profits to continue a steady expansion.

What makes In-N-Out's success surprising are the company practices that would seem to limit its growth. For starters, there is a grand total of four items on the menu—hamburger, cheeseburger, double-double cheeseburger, and French fries—plus soft drinks, shakes, and lemonade, of course. That's it. No dessert, no coffee, no breakfast menu. Nothing else. Instead of variety, the company has kept the same small menu and has delivered it flawlessly for more than 50 years. The only change, if you can call it that, in the last decade was the addition of a new soft drink.

The company's philosophy then and now is: "Give customers the freshest, highest quality foods you can buy and provide them with friendly service in a sparkling clean environment."[1] Nothing In-N-Out serves is ever frozen. Nothing sits under a heat lamp—in fact, the restaurants don't have heat lamps. Nor does it have a microwave or a freezer. Everything is cooked to order, which means customers have to wait a bit longer for their food, but they don't seem to mind. The hamburgers are delicious, and as the long lines attest to, it's worth the wait.

Instead of varying the menu or adding specials, all Harry and Esther's efforts went into quality, freshness, and service. To make sure they have a friendly, well-trained staff, In-N-Out pays well above the industry standard, and rewards top-performing managers with trips to places such as Cancun and Sydney. Its managers average 12 years on the job, compared to just one year for the overall retail food industry (according to the California Restaurant Association), and its hourly workers stay an average of two years, compared to 10 months industry-wide.[2] Esther, who worked in the kitchen in the early days peeling potatoes and making burger patties by hand, has a simple explanation for the higher payroll costs.

"They're the ones you see," Esther said. "They take your orders and make your food. They're so important, so you want to have happy, shining faces working there."[3]

If you ask customers, In-N-Out beats the bigger chains hands down.

In 1997, the first year it was eligible for consideration, a survey in *Restaurants & Institutions* magazine named In-N-Out Burger the best place for burgers nationwide, despite the fact that it was only located in California and Nevada (it's now in Arizona as well).[4] In-N-Out continued its success, as customers selected it best in its category for the next consecutive eight years; the company repeatedly ranked first in food quality, value, service, atmosphere, and cleanliness.[5] The Snyder's original mission of quality, freshness, and service is still working well, and In-N-Out continues to top the charts in all three categories.

"Everyone in the fast-food industry envies In-N-Out," said Carl Karcher, founder of the Carl's Jr. restaurant chain. "We're working on new products every year and In-N-Out keeps the same menu and knocks 'em dead."[6] As In-N-Out Burger has proven, you don't need a big menu and you don't need to constantly change it: doing one thing exceptionally well can build an intensely loyal following.

Stick to Your Guns

An Internet search engine may seem as far removed from hamburgers as you can get, but some of the same problems and principles apply. In Silicon Valley, if you're working at a hot company, you're the ultimate insider. People lucky enough to work at sizzling companies such as Apple, Oracle, Sun Microsystems, or Netscape when they went public were the envy of their friends and neighbors. The same was true for those inside at Amazon (even though it's in Seattle, not Silicon Valley), Yahoo, and eBay: they became instant celebrities when their stocks took off like rockets. Those people who haven't "made it" yet are mostly under the radar, watching from the sidelines as they burn the midnight oil trying to turn their company into the next Silicon Valley success story.

Against this backdrop, one company that was almost completely overlooked in the shadow of eBay and Yahoo went on to become one of the hottest start-ups in Silicon Valley history. What makes it even more remarkable is that the company built its entire fortune on an area that was not only overlooked, but actually dismissed, by all the major players as a "commodity."

Do One Thing Better Than Anyone Else

Larry Page and Sergey Brin didn't set out to become billionaires. That was the furthest thing from their minds when they met as Ph.D. students at Stanford. In fact, they didn't exactly hit it off at first. Sergey, originally from Russia, attended the University of Maryland at College Park, and Larry, from the University of Michigan, couldn't agree on anything, and they debated almost every topic they discussed. One thing they did agree on was a new approach to solving one of the biggest challenges in computing: retrieving relevant information from massive amounts of data.

Internet search was pioneered by another famous pair from Stanford, David Filo and Chih-Yuan "Jerry" Yang, who founded Yahoo as a directory of Websites, and went on to launch the first commercial Internet search engine. Having amassed the lion's share of traffic and eyeballs on the Internet, Yahoo had evolved into a portal by 1998. With 80 million customers a month at the time, Yahoo's market cap was $32 billion, and its stock price had jumped from $28 a share to $386 in 52 weeks.[7] Yahoo was giving away free e-mail, personal ads, and an assortment of services in return for selling ads to captive customers on its Website. Archrival Excite battled Yahoo—and ultimately lost—in the portal wars, and a host of smaller players were vying for a piece of the action.

As Yahoo prospered, it moved further from its roots, relegating Internet search to a smaller role in the quest for unique visitors and page views, which were the metrics of success at the time. Meanwhile, Webmasters around the world quickly learned how to game the system, adding hundreds of extraneous keywords so they would come up in the search results of the major search engines. These keywords were invisible to the viewer, but were indexed by the search engines to rank Websites. Because the search engines counted keywords, the relevance of search results declined as the number of Websites exploded. The system that worked fine for Yahoo in the early days began producing search results that were less and less relevant, and the results were further skewed by a slew of paid listings and banner ads.

As Larry and Sergey watched this scene unfold, they came up with a better idea for Internet search. They collaborated on a paper they published at Stanford in which they laid out the architecture for their new idea. Instead of counting keywords, they developed a system of ranking search results based on the number of backlinks, theorizing that the more sites linked to a given page, the more popular that page must be. They took it a step further, rating the quality of links based on the traffic to that site. In other words, a link from a heavily trafficked site such as MSNBC or CNET was worth more than a link from Joe's Plumbing.

In a move not unlike Michael Dell, they cobbled together a system in Larry's dorm room and maxed out their credit cards to buy a terabyte of memory to set up a server. The two starving students begged and borrowed any parts they could find, often hanging out at the Stanford loading docks to see if they could appropriate any incoming equipment. They named their first prototype search engine Backrub, a tongue-in-cheek reference to backlinks in their new PageRank system. As they refined and improved it, Backrub became popular among the Stanford crowd, but its reach didn't extend much further.

Larry and Sergey were convinced they had superior search technology, but they had no money to fund it. Much like Steve Jobs and Steve Wozniak two decades before, they approached all the major search engines about licensing their technology. Their pitch fell on deaf ears. The big Internet companies were transforming themselves into portals, and they weren't very concerned about providing more relevant search results. If the search was getting 80 percent of the correct results, that was close enough. Even though many of these companies acknowledged that Larry and Sergey had, in fact, built a better mousetrap, they weren't interested in licensing it. Besides, they saw search as a commodity—anybody could do it, and many were.

Larry and Sergey were baffled by that response. They *knew* that search was important, but they couldn't get anybody to listen. Looking ahead, they believed the exponential growth of the Web would make finding relevant results harder as the number of Web pages mushroomed. They weren't interested in becoming a portal; all they wanted to do was deploy their new technology to improve search.[8]

When Jobs and Wozniak failed in trying to license their technology to Hewlett-Packard and got the cold shoulder, they went out on their own and started Apple Computer. Like their famous predecessors, Larry and Sergey also decided to go it alone. In hindsight, the lack of interest in licensing their technology was actually a blessing in disguise. As Larry observed, starting their own company "does seem like a better option than going to work for someone on commercializing a technology that they don't care about."[9]

Even with strong technology, Larry and Sergey had trouble getting attention. At the time, Google was a minnow in the shark tank. With 10,000 searches a day, Google still paled in comparison to the 80 million monthly visitors on Yahoo. At the same time, Excite merged with @Home in an attempt to find a competitive edge, and dozens of other well-funded competitors were all trying to stake their claim in the same area. Larry and Sergey couldn't even pay their credit card bills.

Improving a Commodity

While other Internet companies were riding high, Larry and Sergey got kicked out of their Stanford dorm. Lacking any better options, they moved their fledgling operation into a garage in Menlo Park, California, which was owned by a friend of a friend. They put their Ph.D.s on hold, wrote a business plan, and started pitching investors. With the help of some professors and their contacts, they quickly got the attention of some heavy hitters. Andy Bechtelstein, one of the cofounders of Sun Microsystems, was so impressed with their new technology that he wrote them a check for $100,000 on the spot. They had to wait for a month to cash it, though, because at that point Google didn't even exist outside of a bunch of servers. They officially incorporated in September 1998, ultimately raising $1 million in seed money from family and friends.

Larry and Sergey continued to refine and improve Google, and it grew through word of mouth. By spring of the following year when they moved out of the garage into a real office, Google had grown to half a million searches a day. Their technology got attention on Sand Hill Road, they raised $25 million from venture capital giants Sequoia Capital and Kleiner Perkins, and Michael Moritz and John Doerr joined the board of directors.

A Day Late...

Even with the backing of two prominent venture backers and superior technology, they still had trouble getting others in the industry to pay attention. When they officially launched Google in 1999, there were already dozens of search engines vying for the same attention. In addition to Yahoo, Excite, and America Online, the field was packed with competitors such as AltaVista, Lycos, Inktomi, Ask Jeeves, LookSmart, Northern Light, and GoTo.com. Even Disney had its own search engine/portal named Go. There were dozens of other competitors in an extremely crowded field, and with Internet stocks in the stratosphere, many of those companies were worth billions. By the time Larry and Sergey officially launched Google, Yahoo's market cap was $30 billion, Excite's was $6.9 billion, @Home's was $12 billion, Inktomi's was $4.4 billion, Go2Net's was $1.3 billion, and America Online's was a whopping $128 billion.[10] Google was definitely late to the party.

The other strike against them was their revenue model—or lack of one. As the Internet storm moved through the valley, Google resisted calls to become a portal. Like Harry and Esther Snyder who refused to expand the menu at In-N-Out Burger, Larry and Sergey refused to abandon their principles. The Google site was clean and fast, with no ads, no partner links, and no other revenue-generating services. They put all their eggs in the search basket, with 100 percent of their energy focused on making their search results faster and better. Critics were quick to point out that their fast, clean interface didn't give them a way to actually make money—or so it seemed.

In June 2000, after lining up a string of other partnerships, Google finally succeeded in becoming the search engine for Yahoo's search feature. To show their solidarity, David Filo of Yahoo joined Larry and Sergey for a joint press conference. Despite the partnership with Yahoo and Google's growing popularity, they *still* couldn't get any attention from reporters.

Larry and Sergey made one more masterstroke—so obvious now that nobody saw it coming. In 2001, Google introduced a new type of online ad—small text ads relevant to the search results. The new ads, called AdWords, are particularly effective because they only come up if the customer is already searching for something. The idea was originally introduced by GoTo.com (now Overture) several years earlier, but in a different form. Instead of displaying the paid listings first, which made people question the veracity of the search results, Google's AdWords are on the right side of the page in boxes clearly marked as sponsored ads. The layout is still clean and crisp, and Google is still true to the founders' vision. By waiting to unveil it, they built a big enough base that AdWords was an instant success, and it quickly became a cash machine for Google.

With a laser focus in one area, Larry and Sergey put all their eggs in one basket—doing search incredibly well. When they officially launched the service in 1999, Google indexed about 30 million pages—about the same as the major players. Four years later, Google indexed more than 3 billion Web pages, still delivering results blindingly fast. With a superior search technology—more relevant results and faster speed—Google entered late in a field crowded with competitors and grew into the leading search engine on the Internet.

"Just based on the rationale that search was something that everybody does every day, it seems like focusing on that pretty solidly was going to be a pretty good strategy," Larry explained. "And we were small. It seemed like if we built lots and lots of services, and tried to compete with all those services, that would be a tremendous amount of work. And it's not where our expertise was, either." In the understatement of the decade, he added, "I guess in retrospect it was probably the right decision."[11]

Headed for Extinction

Like Yahoo, another successful Silicon Valley company strayed from its roots, although in this case the company got into serious trouble. In 1999, when everyone else in Silicon Valley was flying high, Borland was voted the company least likely to see the millennium. There was no money in the bank, no new product strategy, and spending was out of control. The company was on the brink of disaster. That is, until Dale Fuller arrived. By returning the company to its roots and focusing all the efforts in one area, Dale brought Borland back from the brink and turned it into a solidly profitable company.

During the 1980s, Borland became one of the legendary Silicon Valley success stories. Started in 1983 by flamboyant Frenchman Philippe Kahn, Borland made software tools such as Turbo Pascal, a revolutionary program that allowed developers to write applications for PCs. Sales quickly rocketed to $500 million a year, and Philippe built a fairy-tale campus in the redwoods in Scotts Valley, California, complete with Japanese-style buildings and koi ponds.

As with many start-ups, early success fostered a feeling of invincibility at Borland, and the company got carried away. Philippe strayed from the company's core strength of building developer tools and made it his personal mission to take on Microsoft, trying to offer an alternative to Microsoft Office. Microsoft ran over Borland like a steamroller. Philippe eventually left the company in 1995, and a series of new CEOs all tried to move the company in different directions, including changing the name of the company from Borland to Inprise. All of them failed.

While Google was just starting out and Amazon, Yahoo, and Excite were fighting to be king of the hill, Borland was a company headed for extinction. By the time Dale Fuller took over as CEO in 1999, things were pretty scary. "The company's 1,100 employees had no direction, and people were walking around like zombies," Dale recalls. "The company had literally no money in the bank, it was burning huge amounts of cash, it had little isolated projects all over the place with no business plan behind any of them. In many cases, they didn't even have a customer in mind. Various teams were just blindly working on different projects with no direction."[12]

By the time Dale arrived, pretty much everybody had given the company up for dead. Not one Wall Street analyst would cover the stock. In fact, the situation was so bad that the company had less than six days of cash left before running out of money. Dale was a veteran of big companies such as Apple and NEC, and he had sold his own start-up to Lycos, so he'd been around the block a few times. Like millions of other people in business, he had always dreamed of being CEO of a big company. In this case, though, it didn't take long before the dream looked a lot more like a nightmare.

The first thing he did was take over the financial reins of the company, instructing his staff to submit every purchase order more than $2 for his approval. "You couldn't buy a pen without me signing for it," he said. While it seemed severe at first, that exercise proved to be enlightening. Spending was out of control in an environment where even the dumbest expenses weren't questioned. For example, the budget included $100,000 a year for chemicals for the fish ponds, but there hadn't been fish in the ponds for 10 years. Raccoons had eaten them all.[13]

Watching the expenses helped slow the bleeding, but the patient was still dying. Out of desperation, Dale played a card that came dangerously close to Philippe Kahn's battle with Microsoft. He knew that

Microsoft was infringing on some of the company's patents, and Microsoft was knee-deep in the government's antitrust trial. He flew to Microsoft headquarters in Redmond, Washington, to confront Microsoft, knowing the last thing it needed at the time was another lawsuit. "I went to Microsoft and said, 'I don't want to sue you. Maybe we can work out a licensing agreement,'" Fuller said.[14] His gambit succeeded. He came back home with a check for $125 million—a $100 million licensing agreement and a $25 million equity investment in the company.

With the immediate crisis averted, Dale sat down with all the product marketing managers. He drew a big line on the white board, breaking it down into quarters going out for four years. He then had each product manager draw on the board to show the timeframe for the projects they were working on. Every single person went up and drew a circle three months out. Every project in the company was only a three-month project. There was nothing past that. "When I took over the company in April, it pretty much was out of business like in June. It was very scary," Dale said. "The company had no vision, it had no way to measure itself, and it had never written down what it was going to go do. No one knew where they were going. They were a ship out to sea, and they were rudderless."

Selling the company was definitely one of the options, and every day that went by it seemed more and more likely that it was the only option left. The company hired three big outside consultants to evaluate strategic options, and the conclusion all three came to was the same: "Find a buyer, quick!"[15]

Despite all the management turmoil, Borland had a strong, core group of dedicated developers. By returning to its roots of building tools for developers, he hoped he could win back the loyalty and support. He refocused the company on its core strength, building developer tools, but with one new requirement—everything the company did in the future had to support the Internet.

He also knew that the future of software development would be the Internet. Based on a strong gut feeling and the company's historical strengths, he put a stake in the ground and said, "Everything that this company is going to focus on is the Internet." The phrase he preached relentlessly inside the company was "nothing but net." He told everyone that if they're working on a project today, they better figure out how it's going to work on the Internet, how it's going to support the

Internet, and how it's going to drive for more applications to be on the Internet. Otherwise, that project will be gone within five months.

For the first time in recent memory, the company had a direction. Although the company's developer base hadn't grown much in the years before Dale arrived, those that remained were devoted to Borland's development tools. With a succession of management teams and no apparent direction over the years, though, Dale knew the company had neglected its core customers. At his first developer's conference in Philadelphia, the convention center ballroom was filled with 2,500 angry and skeptical developers. He needed to win them back, so he apologized to them. "I told them we'd abandoned them, and we'd never do that again."[16]

Nothing but Net

The next major phase Dale worked on was execution, with all efforts now focused on creating Internet tools for the core group of developers. Rather than simply taking on Microsoft by building development tools for Windows, or similarly battling IBM in Linux or Sun in Windows, Dale chose a strategy of navigating between the bigger players. Dale announced that Borland would be a neutral ally—in essence, the Switzerland of software—focusing on interoperability among the competing services. Simply put, Borland's software allows developers to translate applications written for one platform onto competing systems. This is especially important for small developers who don't have the time, money, and resources to build multiple versions of each program.

Borland introduced several new products for developers, including a JBuilder for Apple's Mac OS X, the first new development tool for the Mac in eight years, and a suite of tools for .NET, Microsoft's new development environment.[17] Microsoft's own development tools are written for Windows developers, while Borland's tools provide .NET support to developers in mixed environments.[18] Underlying each new product is Borland's renewed focus on developers and their strategy of focusing on Internet applications. "It's all about developers," Fuller said. "A year and two months ago, we recommitted to really refocus on developers; that's all our business is."[19]

In January 2001, Dale changed the company name back to Borland, signaling that the company's return to its roots was complete. He brought the company back from the brink, chalking up nine successive quarterly increases. The company that was days away from bankruptcy when he arrived three years earlier now had $300 million in the bank, no debt, and the renewed devotion of its dedicated developers.

A Single Focus

All three companies have demonstrated the power of focus instead of trying to be all things to all people. In-N-Out has built an intensely loyal following with the same limited menu for more than 50 years, putting freshness, quality, and service ahead of variety. Google entered late in a crowded field and went on to become the number-one search engine in the world by doing one thing flawlessly—search. Dale Fuller turned Borland around and brought it back to life by focusing on one thing—development tools for its core customers. As all three demonstrate, you can succeed with only one trick up your sleeve, if you do that one thing better than anybody else.

Chapter 6

If You Can't Find a Solution, Change the Problem

No matter how much research and preparation you do, sometimes things just don't go your way. When you're doing everything you can and none of the answers are working, try changing the question. Peter Thiel learned that lesson when he left Wall Street to head back to Silicon Valley in the middle of the Internet boom. The wireless industry was about to explode, and Peter joined forces with Max Levchin to start a new company called Field Link.

The two entrepreneurs were convinced there would be a growing market for encryption technology for wireless devices, but early on they ran into problems. The biggest roadblock was resistance from the wireless carriers. Even though carriers understood the need for security on mobile devices, Field Link was an unproven start-up with no pricing power and no negotiating leverage. There were also dozens of other companies trying to do the same thing, so Field Link needed the carriers more than the carriers needed them.

Another problem was usability. They early wireless browsers were very difficult to use, and Peter and Max couldn't get the kind of functionality on it that they thought customers would want. These frustrated efforts led them in a new direction. Instead of trying to fight two things they couldn't control—the difficult wireless interface and the centralized power of the wireless carriers—they turned their efforts to a simpler arena, sending payments by e-mail.

At the time, there were 140 million people with e-mail in the United States, but only about 2 million people who had Internet-enabled wireless devices. In addition to providing a bigger potential market, the e-mail solution also eliminated the need for big corporate partnerships. Equally important, e-mail gave them a way to present their payment solution in an easy, intuitive format, something they couldn't do with small screens on wireless devices.

They changed the company name to PayPal and launched an e-mail–based payment service. To jump-start it, Peter decided to pay customers $10 when they signed up for PayPal and another $10 for every friend they referred. "At the time it seemed absolutely crazy, but it was a less expensive way to acquire customers," he explained. "And the kind of customers we got were actually much more valuable, because they were using the system a lot. It was better than just getting a million random customers by running an ad campaign."[1]

PayPal was an immediate hit. In the first six months, more than a million people signed up for the new payment service. With its easy, customer-friendly interface, PayPal quickly became the payment system of choice on eBay, and with that, its growth skyrocketed. When they finally decided to shut down the wireless version a year later, there were 4 million customers on PayPal and only 10,000 using the wireless product. Even though eBay had its own in-house payment service called Billpoint, PayPal became the undisputed leader in online payments. PayPal went public, and eBay eventually bought PayPal for $1.5 billion. If Peter and Max had stuck with their original plan, the story would have had a dramatically different outcome.

A Clodhopper by Any Other Name

Sometimes courage means sticking to your plan, and sometimes it means changing it. In the mid-1990s, two best friends decided to go into business together. Their idea was to start a candy company; their secret weapon—grandma's candy recipe. A cluster of graham crackers and cashews with chocolate, vanilla, or peanut butter that was irresistible. Once you try it, it's hard to stop. They loved the candy, and so did everyone else who tried it, so they were convinced it would be a hit.

When Chris Emery and Larry Finnson set out on their new adventure, they had no idea how hard it would be to get their foot in the door.

As they soon discovered, candy is a $24 billion industry in North America, dominated by huge multinational companies such as Hershey and Mars that control 75 percent of the market and have a strong lock on distribution. Just getting shelf space can cost thousands of dollars in "slotting fees" paid to supermarkets and retailers.[2]

Listening to them, Chris and Larry sound like the business version of Bob and Doug Mckenzie on the television satire *Great White North*, constantly interrupting each other, trading good-natured barbs, and generally having a good time. The two were best friends in high school in Winnipeg, Manitoba, and after college, both worked for their fathers—Chris answering phones in his dad's office and Larry building winter roads and ice bridges. They had always daydreamed of starting their own business, and because both of their dads were entrepreneurs, they had plenty of encouragement.

Armed with little more than grandma's candy recipe and a lot of ambition, they struck out on their own. They rented a 700 square foot office and started mixing up 80-pound batches of candy by hand, which they packaged in big plastic jars. With no money for the proper equipment or to hire employees, they did everything themselves. They didn't have distribution agreements, so the two entrepreneurs started hanging out at craft fairs and in shopping malls to hand out samples of their Clodhoppers, much the same way Debbi Fields launched Mrs. Fields Cookies. In an effort to be taken seriously by the bigger players, they named their company Krave's Candy Company, because it sounded official, even though they called the candy Clodhoppers.

Chris and Larry's first break came when they convinced a local distributor to use his Wal-Mart vendor number to get Clodhoppers on the shelves of five local Wal-Mart stores. The candy sold quickly, but the Wal-Mart buyer called and asked, "Who the hell are you and what are you doing in my store?" They set up a meeting with the buyer, and she soon became one of their biggest supporters. They were still shipping candy in big plastic jugs, though, and that didn't really fit the image Wal-Mart wanted to portray. She suggested they package the candy in gift boxes so they would make good holiday gifts. That sounded like a good idea, so they changed gears, and packaged the candy in fancy, embossed boxes like other fine chocolates. With a name like Krave's, they figured that would be a natural fit. Even with her help, though,

Clodhoppers only made it into a handful of local Wal-Mart stores in Canada. They couldn't manage to move further upstream.

Without really thinking about branding or positioning, they intuitively knew that they wanted to target the high end of the candy market. One of the biggest expenses in their finished product was the packaging, and they needed high margins to cover their costs. That strategy had a host of problems, not the least of which was the high cost of laminated and embossed boxes. When customers opened the boxes, they expected to see fancy chocolates, not what looked like a clump of chocolate with nuts in it. To make matters worse, the gift market tends to be very seasonal, with a lot of candy given as gifts during the holidays but not during the rest of the year. Like many entrepreneurs, their sales weren't as big as their ambitions, and the company was soon struggling.

With no better ideas, the two partners lived hand-to-mouth for several years, and they felt like they were pushing a rock uphill. They managed to keep the company afloat—just barely—and it was a constant struggle for survival. Through trial and error, their sales and marketing slowly evolved, but attracting new customers still relied mainly on sampling. Once people tried Clodhoppers, they loved them. Getting people to try it in the first place was the hard part.

Sales were slowly growing, but the company was still losing money. Krave's was a tiny company that wasn't even on the radar of big retailers and distributors. Even with the local Wal-Mart buyer getting them into a handful of local stores, the big retailers weren't taking them seriously. They didn't have the money, resources, or connections to work their way into established distribution. Furthermore, packaging Clodhoppers in an expensive box and selling them under a fancy name just didn't feel right. They just weren't cracking the code.

Much to their surprise, Chris and Larry discovered a silver lining. Although they were convinced they had the best tasting candy available, they noticed that the media stories about the company always talked about the two partners, focusing on the angle of two best friends starting a company with grandma's candy recipe—not focusing on the product. Sure, the candy was great, but that didn't make an interesting story.

After five years of struggling, Chris and Larry realized that they weren't going to win if they kept playing by the same rules. Throwing caution to the wind, they made a bold decision. If they couldn't penetrate the market by positioning Clodhoppers as an expensive, high-end candy, they weren't going to play that game anymore. They abandoned their efforts to target the high end of the market, sidelining both the Krave's name and the expensive embossed packaging. Instead, they rebranded the company as Chris and Larry's Clodhoppers, embracing the fact that they were a small company run by two best friends, instead of trying to act like a big company when they weren't. Instead of a stuffy name and appearance, the new packaging was an inexpensive plastic bag with a fun, friendly label complete with caricatures of Chris and Larry on the front.

The cheaper packaging also let them lower the price, from $5.50 a box to $3.50. Armed with the brand-new image and lower prices, they quickly got the attention of retailers and distributors. They also forged partnerships with Air Canada and WestJet, a regional airline in Canada, exposing another 400,000 people to Clodhoppers.[3] With these successes under their belt, they struck several other promotional deals and continued to build their new brand.

Then Chris and Larry got their big break. They were exhibiting at a Wal-Mart vendor show in Toronto, when a man approached them at the end of the day. They were busy passing out candy and they didn't even read his badge. They introduced themselves: "I'm Chris" and "I'm Larry."

"I'm Lee Scott, president and CEO of Wal-Mart," he said.

"We've been waiting all our lives to meet you!" Larry blurted. Lee liked their samples, and told them to send their candy to Wal-Mart headquarters in Bentonville, Arkansas. They did, and in Christmas 2000, Wal-Mart tested Chris and Larry's Clodhoppers in 400 stores across the United States. Based on their strong sales during the test, their candy was rolled out to all 2,700 stores the next year, which gave them another 40 percent growth for the year."[4]

With the new branding and a new attitude, Chris and Larry's fortunes turned around. In the next two years, sales tripled, the company became solidly profitable, and they locked in agreements with many of the distributors who wouldn't even talk to them before. When their strategy of targeting the high end of the market wasn't working, they changed the problem—embraced their true identity and turned their biggest weakness into their biggest strength. The two partners continue to be best friends, and the story behind the story has helped fuel their success.

Learn From the Past—Don't Live in It

Decisions about future direction are always difficult. The bigger the company, the harder those decisions can be. With more at stake, though, those decisions are even more critical. Ironically, the more successful you've been in the past, the harder it is to let go of it. But when your new strategy isn't working, that's exactly what you have to do.

Chris and Larry's solution of changing their fundamental positioning was much like the problem Ron Shaich faced with Au Bon Pain. Like countless entrepreneurs, Ron started from humble beginnings. After opening a cookie store in Boston, he struck a deal with a nearby bakery to sell croissants for breakfast. Within a year, he and the bakery owner joined forces to start Au Bon Pain.

Watching his customers, Ron dreamed of building a nationwide chain of bakery cafes. "You didn't need a Harvard degree to see the opportunity," the Harvard Business School graduate said. "Customers were coming into the store to buy a baguette and asking me to cut it from top to bottom. Then they'd take luncheon meat they'd just bought from the grocery store next door and make a sandwich."[5]

Ron pursued his dream; he built more than 250 Au Bon Pain restaurants in the Northeast and took the company public in 1991. Although Au Bon Pain was one of the first restaurants to offer high-quality sandwiches with freshly made bread, Ron made two mistakes. First, to keep costs down and prices low, he kept store build-outs to a minimum, with plastic tables and chairs and minimal interior design. Second, he limited store locations to downtown areas. Those locationa were fine during the week, but most downtown areas are ghost towns at night and on weekends, which makes it difficult to attract customers and leads to peaks and valleys in store traffic.

As Au Bon Pain grew to more than 500 locations, Ron noticed a shifting trend in what customers wanted. When he traveled throughout the country, he noticed people were paying more for premium goods. "Instead of Folger's coffee, they were grinding their own coffee beans;

instead of drinking Budweiser, they were buying Samuel Adams beer,"[6] Ron said. He realized that customers were shifting from fast food to more upscale dining. With its no frills décor and cheap interiors, Au Bon Pain wasn't in a position to offer that.

In their groundbreaking book *Trading Up*, Michael Silverstein and Neil Fiske describe eating as an emotional experience. "Wherever they go for their food, middle-market consumers think of eating as more than an exercise in satisfying a hunger or filling up," the authors explain. "They are willing to pay a premium for food that tastes better, looks more appealing, is served in a pleasant environment, and engages them emotionally."[7] Ron Shaich spotted this trend early. Watching the shift in customer behavior, he realized that Au Bon Pain couldn't capitalize on it; the future was in a different direction. The problem he faced was the classic legacy infrastructure. With hundreds of stores, repositioning the company would have been extremely difficult.

Fortunately, the answer was close at hand. Au Bon Pain had acquired the St. Louis Bread Company in 1993. Like Au Bon Pain, the St. Louis Bread Company served sandwiches on freshly baked bread. The entire concept and execution was completely different, though. While Au Bon Pain had cheap, almost sterile interiors in downtown locations, the St. Louis Bread Company restaurants were located in the suburbs with warm, friendly interiors that made the atmosphere much more inviting. This formula was popular with customers, and the 19-store chain was averaging $1.1 million at each location. He fine-tuned the concept to boost sales and renamed it Panera Bread.

At the same time Panera Bread was thriving, Au Bon Pain was feeling the pain. Sales were down, turnover in the stores was high, and the core concept was struggling. Like Chris and Larry, Ron tried everything to find the solution. He ultimately realized that small tweaks wouldn't change the fundamental problem—cheap, sterile interiors and downtown locations—in the face of changing customer desires. He also knew that remodeling and relocating 550 stores, and then trying to reposition them in the marketplace, just wouldn't be practical.

Instead of trying to fix Au Bon Pain, he changed the problem. Ron went to his board of directors and proposed an outlandish idea—sell the existing 550 Au Bon Pain stores, rename the company Panera Bread, and grow the chain of 19 Panera Bread stores into a national brand. At first the board members thought he was joking. When they realized he was serious, it very nearly cost him his job. Although skeptical, it was hard to argue with the numbers, and the board eventually went along with it. The analysts on Wall Street weren't exactly supportive, and the stock was pounded after Ron announced his new strategy.

By 1999, the company sold all 550 Au Bon Pain locations to an investor group, and put all its effort into Panera Bread. Learning from his past mistakes, Ron made two significant changes with Panera Bread. First, instead of the low-cost décor, he invested heavily in store design to make it warm, friendly, and inviting. Second, he abandoned the downtown shopping areas in favor of the suburbs. After that, he stuck to his tried-and-true formula—providing high-quality meat on freshly baked bread.[8] The restaurants also offer soups, salads, and baked goods, served on china with silverware. The menu includes upscale sandwiches such as Asiago roast beef, smokehouse turkey, and Tuscan chicken, all served on a variety of freshly baked bread.

In addition to great food, the ambience is key to Panera's success. With the warm, friendly décor and upbeat personality, Panera Bread was an instant hit. The company even added free wireless Internet access to encourage customers to linger. In addition to drawing flocks of people during mealtimes, there is a steady stream of people coming in throughout the afternoon.

"People want real food. They want it served by real people in an environment that engages them. And it's our bread that roots our ability to do that. I mean, this is real bread, done in an authentic way, and following the traditions of bakers that have done this for hundreds of years, on stone deck ovens."[9]

Ron's "bet the farm" gamble paid off. Panera Bread went on to become the biggest bakery-restaurant chain in the country, with more than 550 locations and $1 billion in sales in 2003.[10] The same analysts who initially criticized Ron's plan were soon lavishing praise on the company, and comparing Panera Bread to some of the hottest names in the food industry, including Starbucks and Krispy Kreme.[11] Believing he couldn't solve two fundamental problems—store ambience and location—he changed the problem entirely. By sacrificing his original vision and learning from his mistakes, he moved firmly into the future with Panera Bread.

Blockbuster Problems

Ron Shaich's bold gamble with Panera Bread may be an extreme example, but it's a very instructive one. All too often people get trapped by their current surroundings and locked into their current strategy, even if it isn't working. Like Au Bon Pain, Blockbuster Video faced a problem of a changing marketplace and a formula for growth that seemed to be fraying at the edges. With 6,000 stores around the globe, the problems at Blockbuster were on a much larger scale.

Shortly after Viacom bought Blockbuster Video, the video rental giant was in disarray. The new CEO moved the corporate headquarters to Dallas to end the influence of Wayne Huizinga, and consequently, many of the senior managers left the company. Sales plummeted, Wall Street pounded Viacom stock, and the CEO subsequently left the company. The video giant was at a crossroads, and Viacom CEO Sumner Redstone jumped in to try to turn it in the right direction.

As he got a crash course about the business, Sumner quickly realized the underlying economics of the video rental business were extremely unfavorable. When a new movie was released on video, rental companies had to pay the studios $65 for each tape up front. Renting a tape for $3, the company would break even on the tape after 22 rentals, not including overhead. In order to guarantee enough demand to make a profit, though, the rental chain had to cut back on the number of tapes in the initial purchases. Because the demand for new releases starts high and quickly tapers off, retailers couldn't justify buying enough tapes to meet the initial demand.[12]

Like every other video rental chain, Blockbuster found itself in the same dilemma, but on a much larger scale. By paying $65 for each video, with 10,000 videos in each store and 6,000 stores in the chain, Blockbuster was paying $3.9 billion to the studios *in advance*. The studios were quite happy with this arrangement and had no incentive to change, but the economics were killing Blockbuster.

The flip side of the coin was that when a new movie came out on video, too many customers would go home empty-handed. This was consistently a major customer complaint. Executives at Blockbuster called this "managed dissatisfaction," trying to balance cash flow and profitability with disappointed customers.[13] This strategy clearly wasn't working and Blockbuster was suffering, with 30 percent of its customers walking out the door empty-handed.[14]

Blockbuster faced a Catch-22. It could simply buy more videos up front, which would keep customers happy at the expense of profits. Or it could cut back on the video purchases, which would improve profits (in the short term) but disappoint more customers and hurt its position in the long run. "In those days, customers never got what they wanted," Sumner recalled. "It was like going to McDonald's and asking for a hamburger and being told they only had French fries."[15]

Sumner hired John Antioco from Taco Bell as the new Blockbuster CEO, and the two proposed a novel solution—sharing revenues from video rentals with the studios. Instead of paying the studios a flat fee of $65 up front, they proposed paying a small up-front fee and giving the studios 40 percent of the rental. In return, Blockbuster would triple the number of movies it ordered. Customers would win because they wouldn't go home empty-handed, and Blockbuster would win because it would kill two birds with one stone—improving cash flow and increasing sales. And the studios would win—they hoped—by ultimately making more money.

Knowing it would be tough to sell the idea to the movie studios, John simulated a revenue-sharing agreement in six test markets, buying more videos up front as an experiment. Acting as if the stores were no longer limited on purchases, they could make customers a novel promise—new releases would be guaranteed in stock. The test was a huge success, and Blockbuster went back to Hollywood armed with data to back up its new plan. Disney quickly signed up for the plan, and Viacom owned Paramount; the other studios soon got on board. There was also an added bonus. Because the studios were now getting 40 percent of the rentals, they had incentive to put their marketing muscle behind the video release date to increase demand, a practice that was nonexistent before revenue sharing. Finally, when demand for new movies decreased, Blockbuster could sell the used tapes to consumers and recoup their original investment.

The new strategy quickly triggered a dramatic turnaround. Same store rentals were up 10 percent the following year, and Blockbuster's share of the rental market increased from 25 percent to 30 percent in less than six months. "Instead of stocking only 30 tapes of a hit movie in each store, we're stocking 100," Sumner said. "Blockbuster's happy, the studios are happy, and the consumers are happy because they get what they want."[16]

Blockbuster wasn't the only winner. According to industry analysts, the new revenue-sharing model increased the total revenue in the video industry by 7 percent.[17] Changes in technology later mitigated this development as cheaper DVDs arrived, but the lesson still applies. Instead of playing by the same rules that had thwarted video rental companies for years, Sumner Redstone and John Antioco came up with an innovative solution that completely changed the game.[18]

Change the Question

After trying, and failing, to compete in the high end of the market, Chris Emery and Larry Finnson turned their Clodhoppers into a hit by changing the brand's image to embrace their roots.

Although they were in different industries with very different businesses, both Blockbuster Video and Au Bon Pain were mature companies watching their core business deteriorating. Both took drastic actions—Blockbuster changed its business model, and Au Bon Pain changed its entire business. When the problem you're facing in business seems insurmountable and you can't find the answer, it may be time to ask a different question.

Chapter 7

When Something Goes Right, Do It Again

Some of the best ideas for new products or services really aren't new ideas at all. Rather than starting from scratch, you might find it more profitable to come up with new variations on an old model. Consumer products companies have known this for years. Instead of building awareness for a new brand from the ground up, it's less risky to introduce variations of tried-and-true brands. The next time you walk through the grocery store, you'll see what I mean. Building on the proven market for Cheerios, General Mills introduced Honey Nut Cheerios, Multigrain Cheerios, and even Frosted Cheerios, while Post turned the tried-and-true Grape Nuts into Grape Nuts Flakes and Grape Nuts O's.

This approach makes a lot of sense. Customers are more likely to take a chance on a new variation of a familiar brand. After all, if you like Cheerios, there's not much risk in trying Honey Nut Cheerios. Furthermore, the existing marketing efforts for Cheerios can reinforce the new variations at a fraction of the cost of introducing a new brand. This can play out to all logical extremes—and it does. The same idea is true for business in general. Coming up with a new spin on an old idea can increase revenues, decrease costs, and give advertisers, partners, and customers more confidence in your company. By taking a new look at an old idea, you can turn your past success into a gold mine.

If at First You *Do* Succeed...

Gert Boyle never planned to run a company. As a housewife and mother of three, her husband, Neil, was running Columbia Sportswear, the small family business her father originally started as a hat company. Then tragedy struck. In 1970, Neil died of a heart attack at the age of 47, leaving his wife and children a company that was heavily in debt.

The day after Neil's funeral, the phones at the company started ringing off the hook, and the rumor spread quickly that the company was going out of business. Although Gert had a degree in sociology from Arizona State University, she had no business experience whatsoever. With no other options, she stepped in and took over the company. Not surprisingly, the bankers weren't enthusiastic about a housewife trying to run the business, but she persisted. She had to fight the same battles inside the company, too. Some senior managers weren't excited about working for a woman, and they constantly sniped at her, saying, "That's not how Neil would do it."

After two years of flagging sales, the numbers were going in the wrong direction. Columbia had $800,000 in revenues when she took over, which declined to $600,000 a year later. The bankers were growing increasingly nervous, and at that point, they insisted she sell the business. She went along with it, but when they finally found a buyer, it was a lousy deal. When they actually sat down to sign the papers, Gert realized that after paying off the bank loans, she would get just $1,400. She shot back, "For that amount, I can run it into the ground myself."

That was a pivotal point for Gert. She decided on the spot that she was going to do it her way. First, she fired the people who had been fighting her inside the company—including her accountant, lawyer, and general manager. "After that, things went a lot better because I didn't have to fight internally," she recalls. "We hired people that had the same vision we did. You can't have internal people fighting you every inch of the way."

By that point the company was in survival mode. Gert and the other managers cut their salaries to just $500 a month. Then they cut anybody they didn't absolutely need. After that, they dug in their heels and held on. To keep the bankers at bay, she put up the deed to the building as collateral to buy more time. When she paid the note off later, she got the deed back. In the next few years, she repeated this process several times.

Her son Tim, who was in his senior year of college at the time, took off a couple days every month to help out. After graduating, he returned home to work full time at Columbia. Having him there was a godsend to Gert. In addition to having someone to help share the burden of running the company, Tim was plugged into the taste of a younger generation. "When was the last time your mother bought you something you really liked?" Gert points out. "It took a young kid to know what young kids would wear. Remember in the 70s styles changed. It was no longer navy blue pants and blazers."[1]

In the years that followed, Gert and Tim tried everything they could think of to keep the company moving ahead. To increase sales, they made private label clothing for catalogs and retailers, including Eddie Bauer, L.L. Bean, and Orvis. They were one of the first companies to work with Gore in manufacturing Gore-Tex jackets. Their core customers, though, were hunters and fisherman. In the early 1980s, they came up with an idea that would change the course of the company—a coat with a removable liner.

The idea behind this new coat was simple. When you go hunting, you have to dress warmly when you go out at 4 or 5 o'clock in the morning and it's freezing cold. After the sun comes up, it's too warm to wear the same heavy clothing. You can't take off the outside because it's camouflage, so you take the liner out to keep cool. Gert and Tim called it a Quad Parka because it could be worn four different ways. It featured a weatherproof outer jacket and an insulated inner shell that could be worn together or separately. In essence, each parka was really three or four garments in one.

The Quad Parka was a hit with their customers, and it was a steady seller in their niche market of hunters and fishermen. Based on their success with the Quad Parka, Gert and Tim decided to apply the same principle, later called the Columbia Interchange System, to introduce a ski jacket with a removable liner. Skiers were a completely different demographic group than hunters and fishermen; they had different lifestyles and they shopped in different places, but they shared a similar problem—staying warm when it's cold out, without overheating due to exertion. They called the new jacket the Bugaboo Parka, adding zip-off sleeves and a patented double-zipper to separate the lining from the outer shell.

Gert and Tim made another smart move with the Bugaboo. They didn't try to elbow their way into the already crowded field of high-end apparel against well-entrenched brands such as Patagonia, The North Face, Helly Hansen, Marmot, and Mountain Hardware. All of these competitors already offered expensive, high-functionality sportswear, and it would be tough to take them on. Columbia took a different approach with the Bugaboo, offering a high-quality, stylish jacket at a substantially lower price. In addition to sporting an innovative design, the Bugaboo cost about $100 less than comparable jackets.[2]

The Bugaboo was an immediate hit. Columbia has now sold more than 4 million Bugaboos, making it the single most successful jacket in the history of the ski apparel industry. It also spawned a host of copycats, and 3-in-1 jackets are now commonplace in the apparel industry.

While the Interchange System and the Bugaboo were the company's breakout products, it was a new ad campaign that really put Columbia on the map. Before 1984, all of Columbia's ads focused on the quality of their products. That was an important message for a traditional ad, but it just wasn't very exciting. When their ad agency—Borders, Perrin, and Norrander (BPN)—proposed that Gert should star in Columbia's ads, Tim quipped, "My mother the supermodel." The creative team at BPN persisted, and finally convinced them to go along with the idea. After all, they pointed out, how many other companies are run by a mother-and-son team?

In Columbia's ad campaign, Gert plays the cantankerous "Mother Boyle," an overbearing taskmaster who ruthlessly tests the versatility and durability of Columbia garments—often at Tim's expense—making sure that each product can stand up to her tough standards and Oregon's legendary bad weather. In one commercial, Tim wears a waterproof jacket while she pours a watering can over his head. In another, Mother Boyle retorts, "Don't forget who makes the pants in the family." This campaign earned Columbia the coveted Marketing Innovation award at the 1997 Super Show, an international sporting goods and apparel trade show. Since the introduction of Bugaboo and the launch of the Mother Boyle ad campaign, Columbia's sales have skyrocketed, growing from $13 million in 1983 to $760 million in 2001.[3]

After their initial success with the Bugaboo ski jacket, Gert and Tim again built on their success, introducing a line of boots called

Bugabootoos in 1983. Since then, they've sold more than a million pairs of Bugabootoos, and Columbia now has six different footwear collections.[4] Having established a strong brand, Columbia now even licenses underwear, backpacks, watches, and sunglasses.

Small Improvements Can Produce Big Results

You don't have to come up with a new idea to introduce something new. Successive improvements building on past experience may actually produce better results. In fact, a series of smaller refinements often leads to that big breakthrough. Callaway Golf is best known for introducing the Big Bertha, the club that changed the face of golf. The Big Bertha really wasn't that big of an innovation, though. Most of the advances and improvements were actually made in designing an earlier club, which paved the way for Big Bertha's success.

While Gert and Tim Boyle were building on their success at Columbia, a similar story was taking place 2,000 miles to the south. Ely Callaway had already retired twice before beginning the most exciting part of his business career. First he retired as president of Burlington Industries, Inc., then the world's largest textile company, and started a winery in Southern California. Bucking conventional wisdom that said Southern California could never produce good wines, Callaway Wines turned out to be quite a success. In 1981, he sold the vineyard for $9 million and retired again.

As Ely was enjoying his retirement and playing golf, he saw a hickory-shafted wedge and putter that looked like the beautiful wood-shafted clubs he had used as a child. These clubs weren't antiques, though. They had a steel shaft inside the hickory, and after playing with them, Ely thought, "The feel was absolutely different from anything else ever in golf." Two weeks later, he bought half of Hickory Stick, U.S.A., the small, struggling company that made those specialty putters and wedges, and renamed it Callaway Hickory Stick, U.S.A.[5]

During the next few years, the company grew slowly and steadily. Like Columbia, success didn't come overnight. Ely applied one of his secrets of success earlier in his career—think big and hire smart people. He recruited Richard Helmstetter, a designer of billiard cues in Japan, to be chief club designer, and he steadily carved out a niche making high-performance golf equipment. In 1988, Callaway bought out his partners, changed the company's name to Callaway Golf Company and relocated it to Carlsbad, just north of San Diego.[6]

The same year, the company introduced a new set of irons with a revolutionary club head design that shifted the weight to the club's effective hitting area. The following year, Callaway introduced its first metal woods, the S2H2. They were traditional sized, but with a radical new four-faceted design, which again changed the center of gravity to improve the feel of the club. This small change was actually a very big deal. By the end of 1989, the S2H2 driver was number one on the Senior PGA Tour, and Callaway's sales grew to $21.5 million.

At that point, Ely could have stopped and had a very respectable business; but anyone who follows golf knows that didn't happen. Instead of resting on his laurels, or retiring yet again, Callaway continued building on his success. In the early 1990s, Richard and his research and development group developed a way to create a stainless steel driver that had a larger and more forgiving head than any previous design. It was built on the successful design elements of the S2H2, changing the center of gravity to improve the feel. The major difference was that it had a substantially larger club head with a bigger sweet spot, making it easier to hit the ball longer and straighter than other clubs. Ely named the club "Big Bertha," after a World War I German cannon famous for firing at long ranges.

Ely was convinced he had a winner the first time he took a swing with it. "I knew that if a 72-year-old man could hit this driver off the ground, that anybody could hit it off the tee," Callaway said. He was so confident in the new club that he ordered a whopping 300,000 club heads from the casting company, financing the purchase with his own money. "Prior to Big Bertha, the most feared, shunned, disliked golf club in most everybody's bag was the driver. We made the driver easier to hit. We took the fear out of it."[7]

Sales jumped to $54 million in 1991 and $132 million by 1992, and Big Bertha Drivers were also number one on the Senior PGA, the LPGA, and the Hogan (later renamed Nike) Tours. "With the creation of the Big Bertha Driver, we did something important," said Callaway. "We changed most golfers' attitude toward their driver from one of fear of disdain to one of pleasure."

With a winner on his hands, Callaway Golf continued to make refinements and improvements to its lineup, and Ely kept looking for new ways to make the game more fun for the average golfer. In 1994, the company introduced Big Bertha Irons, and sales increased to $448 million. In 1995, Callaway once again introduced a new variation of the Big Bertha line, launching a new generation called the Great Big Bertha Titanium Driver. This new club had the same larger head and longer shaft of the original Big Bertha, but had a lighter overall weight. Sales increased to $553 million, and Callaway Golf became the number-one maker of both woods and irons. The company made five new product introductions in 1996, following up in 1997 with the Biggest Big Bertha Titanium Driver and the Great Big Bertha Tungsten Titanium Irons in 1997. Annual sales reached $843 million.

By constantly improving and building on his success, Ely Callaway took a small, struggling maker of specialty wedges and built it into the world's largest golf equipment company. When something went right, he did it again. Having built on the advancements in the S2H2, he introduced the Big Bertha and changed the entire golf industry. He added product after product—improving and refining and building on previous success. In the process, he grew a tiny $7 million company into an $800 million operation.

Plan for a Second Act

If you anticipate success—which you should—then you should also be thinking about the sequel early in the game. What can you do now to pave the way for continued success in the future? When Richard Tait and Whit Alexander launched Cranium, they expected a small market for add-on cards for the game. Traditionally, the add-on sales market is very small for games, and neither Trivial Pursuit nor Pictionary ever really managed to break through the resale of card packs. Richard and Whit built a computer model that forecasted the amount of new content they would need based on the average number of players, the number of cards used in the game, and the average roll of the die. They calculated that they had enough content in one Cranium game to last through three holiday seasons, assuming that people play board games two to four times a year at family gatherings.

Soon after launching Cranium, Richard and Whit started to get e-mail from customers who were playing Cranium eight times in a weekend, and the duo quickly realized they would need more content. They introduced add-on card packs called booster boxes. In the first year they sold 1.2 million Cranium games, and they also sold more than 120,000 booster boxes. They were pleasantly surprised to discover that one in eight Cranium customers buys add-on games within three months of buying the game, which is unprecedented in the industry.

In another departure from tradition, Richard and Whit also reinforced their success in a different direction. While they wanted Cranium to represent a celebration of human talents in a box, they also wanted it to be a celebration of cultures. Instead of just selling the American version around the world—an approach that other game makers have used—they went to great lengths to create games that are culturally specific. The British version of Cranium, for example, is written by and for British people, and really celebrates being British. It has a British sense of humor and it's tailored to the interests of the British people. This approach struck a chord, and Cranium was profitable in Britain within four weeks of going on sale there. They took the same approach for their Canadian and French Canadian versions, and Cranium quickly became the number-one selling game in Canada.[8] Cranium continued to reinforce its success, launching additional country specific versions in Australia, Germany, and Japan.

Create a New Spin on an Old Idea

Finding ways to reinforce success isn't always as obvious or immediate as Gert and Tim's introduction of a new ski jacket or Ely's improvement of an existing golf club. It can also mean applying a successful idea to a completely new product, or even a new industry. This is exactly what John Osher did to revolutionize the dental hygiene business.

John had already started three other businesses when he founded a toy manufacturing company called Cap Toys. With a solid background in the industry and a track record of hit toys under his belt, he felt confident in his new venture. When his first two products at Cap Toys failed, though, he nearly went out of business. He hung on, and his next product, Arcade Basketball, was a big hit. Cap Toys not only recovered, but was profitable for the next 10 years. Among its other hits, John and

Cap Toys created Stretch Armstrong, Giant Bubble Gun, and Spin Pop, a lollipop attached to a battery-powered handle that makes the lollipop spin. When Hasbro bought Cap Toys in 1997, it was a happy ending for a company that narrowly averted disaster right out of the gate.

After selling Cap Toys, John took some time off, but he was still "toying" with ideas for new products. To create Spin Pop, he had teamed up with the principals of a Cleveland industrial design firm, John Spark and John Nottingham, along with Lawrence Blaustein, their in-house lawyer. John still owned the patent for Spin Pop, and he was convinced that their knowledge of tiny motors and experience with spinning technology could be valuable. The question was: what could they do with it? As they were kicking around ideas, they wandered the aisles of the local Wal-Mart looking for inspiration. As they walked down the toothbrush aisle, the proverbial light bulb came on. All the electric toothbrushes on sale were $50 or more. If they could make a tiny motor cheap enough to put in a lollipop, why not put it in an electric toothbrush?

In 1998, John and his partners formed a new company, Dr. Johns Products, Ltd., and spent the next 18 months designing and developing an electric toothbrush. The first thing they did was toss conventional wisdom out the window. For starters, they didn't want to charge more than $5, with batteries included. They knew they couldn't afford advertising without driving up the price, so they designed a package that said, "Try Me!" with a switch that let customers try it in the store. After manufacturing the first batch, they started selling it to local retailers.[9]

Starting with a local discount chain, they steadily signed up retailers. Customers loved it, and SpinBrush was an immediate hit. As they built a track record, they landed bigger accounts with national retailers such as Walgreens and Wal-Mart. Defying conventional wisdom, they sold more than 10 million SpinBrushes in 2000—three times as many as all other electric toothbrushes combined—all without running a single ad.[10]

In January 2001, Procter & Gamble (P&G) bought the company for $165 million, with an additional earn-out for the partners based on future sales. P&G took two unprecedented steps: It hired John and two of his partners for three years to keep the company from "screwing it up." And it didn't advertise SpinBrush for the first seven months. P&G quickly rolled out SpinBrush in 35 countries, which was its fastest product launch ever. In March 2002, P&G bought out the founders, which accelerated their earn-out.

Even though it was a brand-new product in a different industry, John and his partners applied their knowledge and experience in small motors and gears to hit a home run. By building on their previous success with the Spin Pop, they parlayed a $1.5 million investment in SpinBrush into a $450 million payout.

Look for Ways to Reinforce Success

Ely Callaway didn't invent the game of golf. He didn't even invent the metal wood. But he continually looked for ways to make the game more fun for the average golfer. By repeatedly building on his success, Ely changed the game of golf forever. Nor did Gert and Tim Boyle invent the ski jacket. They applied their success in hunting jackets in a new direction, and in the process, they made the most successful jacket in the history of the ski apparel industry. John Osher didn't invent the electric toothbrush, but his SpinBrush outsold all other electric toothbrushes combined 3-to-1, all with no advertising. In all three cases, they simply took their secret for success and applied it again.

Both Ely and Gert were relative small fries in their respective industries. Both took over small, struggling companies with well-entrenched competitors. And both slowly and steadily built their companies by refining, improving, and reinforcing their earlier success. Neither Gert nor Ely stumbled across a "lucky break" that catapulted them into fame and fortune. Instead, they both had small successes first—Ely's S2H2 and Gert's Quad Parka. John Osher wasn't even a player in the dental hygiene business when he decided to make an electric toothbrush, but he did know about tiny motors and spinning technology, and he knew how to build things at a low cost.

Applying your past experiences and building on your success can be the best way to succeed again in the future. As legendary Alabama football coach Bear Bryant said, "Most coaches study the films when they lose. I study them when we win—to see if I can figure out what I did right."

Chapter 8

Be Your Own Best Promoter

Nicholas Graham built JOE BOXER into a nationally recognized brand after discovering the power of free publicity. You don't have to pull the kinds of crazy stunts Nick did such as dressing up as the queen of England—or showing up nearly naked in Times Square, like his partner in crime Richard Branson—to promote your company. At the same time, you can't simply run an ad and expect customers to beat a path to your door. With the exponential increase in advertising, there are simply too many advertisers trying to get their message across in an increasingly noisy environment. Unless you have a huge war chest to spend on advertising, you need to think smarter and come up with creative ways to spread the word.

Chris Emery and Larry Finnson were already supplying their Clodhoppers candy to Dairy Queen in Canada to use in Blizzards, but they wanted to get it into the U.S. stores. Having survived after nearly going under, things were finally going well and Chris and Larry were looking to grow their company. Despite their success with Dairy Queen in Canada, they couldn't even get anyone from the Dairy Queen corporate office to return their calls. Then they heard about an upcoming Dairy Queen franchisee convention in Nashville, and even though they weren't franchisees, they decided to attend. Then they got another idea. Dairy Queen was holding an auction for a day with Chuck Mooty, the CEO. The auction was intended to let franchisees bring Chuck to their stores, shake hands, and make Blizzards. But Chris and Larry realized that the rules didn't say that. Anybody could bid—and they did.

When the auction started, the "two guys from Canada" ran away with it. They created a media sensation when they won the bidding at $6,500, with all proceeds benefiting the Children's Hospital Foundation in Winnipeg, Manitoba. "Everybody was saying 'who *are* those guys?!'" Larry said with a laugh.[1] Even though they had to buy their way in, they finally got the attention inside Dairy Queen's corporate office—and their own blizzard of free publicity in the process.[2]

An Easy Way to Get Attention

When Stelios Haji-Ioannou launched easyJet at Luton Airport, which is north of London, he didn't have much money to promote it, so he used some classic guerilla marketing techniques. He dressed crew members in orange sweatshirts and painted the company's phone number on the side of the plane in huge, orange numbers, effectively turning the planes into flying billboards.[3] He kept costs down and focused on "sweating the assets," turning the planes around quickly to maximize efficiency, combined with a sophisticated yield management system that lets the company set prices based on demand.

EasyJet got off to a strong start and steadily expanded, adding more planes and more cities. Three years later, Stelios got a call from the CEO of British Airlines (BA) who invited him to tea and asked if BA could invest in easyJet. Like any small company courted by a powerful competitor, Stelios was flattered, and he knew intuitively what BA's backing could do for easyJet. They discussed an equity investment, and Stelios opened his books to BA, sharing detailed financial and operational information. British Airlines abuptly terminated the talks, and the media soon reported that BA was planning to launch its own discount airline to compete with easyJet and Ryanair. Dubbed "Operation Blue Sky," British Airways planned its new airline "Go" as a blocking strategy to protect its home base from other discounters.[4] From his vantage point, it was clear to Stelios that BA never had any intention of investing in easyJet to begin with—it was just a ploy to get confidential information.

Stelios was steamed. He could take it to court, but he knew that would be a long, expensive battle, and it would be difficult to prove. Instead, he launched his own creative counterattack, buying 10 tickets on Go's inaugural flight from London to Rome. When Go CEO Barbara Cassani got wind of the plan, she deadpanned, "We're very excited that Go is the choice of the low-fares industry."[5] When Stelios and nine cohorts showed up for the Go flight dressed in easyJet's signature orange jumpsuits, they created an uproar by handing out 150 letters promising free flights on easyJet. The Go CEO found herself alone while the reporters piled into the back of the plane to interview Stelios.[6]

After effectively taking over the maiden flight of Go, Stelios used creative publicity to get easyJet out of other tight spots. When travel agents in Greece took easyJet to court for selling airline tickets directly to consumers online, Stelios promised to give a free ticket to anyone who showed up outside the courthouse to cheer him on, guaranteeing plenty of attention in the media.[7]

In a delicious twist of irony, Stelios once again shared headlines with its rival. Three years after launching its discount airline, British Airways spun off Go as a separate company, and easyJet promptly made an offer to acquire it. EasyJet bought Go for £374 million,[8] and Stelios got his payback—and vaulted over Ryanair to become the leading discount airline in Europe.

What Are They Afraid Of?

When Ben Cohen and Jerry Greenfield learned that Pillsbury was demanding that its distributors stop carrying Ben & Jerry's ice cream if they wanted to continue selling Häagen-Dazs, Ben and Jerry immediately got their lawyers on the case. The cofounders of Ben & Jerry's also took their case to the public, mounting a very vocal campaign to embarrass Pillsbury into changing its ways. Jerry started a one-man picket campaign outside Pillsbury headquarters in Minneapolis with a sign and flyers that said, "What's the Doughboy Afraid Of?" Ben & Jerry's put labels on its pints of ice cream with an 800-number that customers could call to get a "What's the Doughboy Afraid Of?" T-shirt and bumper sticker, and the company put up billboards and bus signs in Boston that said, "Don't Let Pillsbury Put the Squeeze on Ben & Jerry's."[9]

Ben & Jerry's got a wave of publicity for its case, including articles in the *New York Times*, *Wall Street Journal*, *San Francisco Chronicle*, *New Yorker*, and *Boston Globe*. Although getting top-notch legal help ultimately ended Pillsbury's attempt to freeze it out of the market, Ben

85

& Jerry's guerilla marketing campaign was a key factor in getting it to the table with a settlement. After Pillsbury spent millions to create a positive image, Ben and Jerry were publicly trashing it with their Doughboy campaign at every opportunity. The two hippies from Vermont not only won the battle, but they got millions of dollars worth of free publicity in the process.[10]

Stelios used this tactic years later when he ran into trouble in Europe. With easyJet off to a strong start, he built on his success by opening easyCar, a discount car rental company that was a natural companion to his discount airline. When easyCar opened in the Netherlands, it ran an ad that said, "The best reason to use easyCar.com can be found at hertz.nl." Hertz lodged a formal complaint about the ad, so Stelios and a cadre of easyCar employees put on their trademark orange jumpsuits again and picketed outside a Hertz location in Amsterdam with signs that read, "What is Hertz afraid of?"[11] The pickets got far more attention than the ad, and like Ben and Jerry, Stelios put himself squarely in the middle of the media spotlight.

Building the Buzz

When Dave Gold opened his first 99 Cents Only store, he knew he had to have some way to get attention for the grand opening, but he couldn't afford an expensive ad campaign. Besides, it was a 99-cent store—it had to look like a bargain. Instead of running an expensive ad in the newspaper, he printed up flyers and created his own hook—he sold televisions for only 99 cents to the first 13 customers (because he opened on the 13th). Then he got his family and friends to call the radio and TV stations and breathlessly announce that there was a crazy event going on at a new store that was selling televisions for 99 cents!

It worked. Dave's grand opening got a lot of media coverage, and the new store got off to a strong start. As the company grew, he changed the tactic slightly, giving away televisions and microwave ovens to the first 99 customers, scooters to the next 99 customers, and so on.[12] When each of those 99 customers told their family and friends what an incredible bargain they got, they became promoters for the store. Now customers stand in line for two or three days before a new store opens, an event that becomes a story in itself.

Richard Tait and Whit Alexander used a different kind of publicity to help launch Cranium. They knew the best way to get people hooked on their new game was to get them to try it. Like Debbi Fields handing out free samples of her cookies in Stanford Shopping Center or Ben & Jerry's giving out free samples of Chunky Monkey or Cherry Garcia in supermarkets, the biggest challenge was getting people to try it.[13] While play tests were a great convincer to get purchasing agents on board, they were too limited by nature—after all, only eight people can play at a time—so they needed something bigger to introduce Cranium to the masses.

Because television ads were too expensive, Richard and Whit borrowed a tactic that Trivial Pursuit had used years earlier. For only $15,000, they recruited 110 disk jockeys from radio stations around the country to read Cranium questions on the air. Callers with the correct answer won a Cranium game. Radio stations love contests because they keep people listening, and it gave them something a little more creative than the usual call-in for concert tickets. As Richard pointed out, what better way to introduce people to Cranium than hearing a clever question or two on the air?[14]

Create Your Own Demand

Another way to get a new product off the ground without a big advertising budget is to create your own demand. When John Johnson launched his new magazine *Negro Digest* during World War II, he funded the first printing by preselling subscriptions. He knew he had to sell more copies to cover his costs, but the biggest magazine distributor in Chicago wouldn't carry it. Instead of giving up, John recruited friends to visit newsstands all over the city to ask for the magazine every day for a week.

When the distributor finally called back to place a small order, John gave the same friends money to go buy copies from the newsstands. The distributor called again and placed a larger order. Seeing the opportunity, the news dealers started aggressively promoting his new magazine, and John went back to the press to print another 5,000 copies. The Chicago distributor quickly became one of his biggest supporters, and within three months, *Negro Digest* was carried in New York and California, selling 50,000 copies a month nationally.[15]

When he later founded *Ebony* and *Jet*, John used the same tactic to boost circulation in Philadelphia and New York. "The reason I succeeded was that I didn't know it was impossible to succeed," John explains in his autobiography *Succeeding Against the Odds*. "If I'd known then what MBAs know now, I would have realized that I couldn't start a business that way. For me, then, ignorance was a blessing. Since I didn't know it was impossible to do what I wanted to do, I did it."[16]

Grassroots Marketing Campaign

Sheryl Leach used a similar tactic to create demand when she entered a new industry with no experience. A former teacher and freelance writer, Sheryl was frustrated that her 2-year-old son wasn't interested in anything for more than five minutes—except a children's video, *We Sing Together*. She tried to buy a follow-up to the video but there wasn't one. Recognizing the opportunity, she decided to make a children's video herself. Her first idea was to make a teddy bear that came to life to play with children. When she saw how captivated her son was by dinosaurs, she changed her plan, and Barney the dinosaur was born.

When Sheryl founded Lyrick Corp. to bring Barney to life, she had no experience producing videos, so she relied on common sense. Her father-in-law had a video studio, and she wrote the script and hired local actors to play the parts. She also did her homework, identifying 17 key elements to make Barney appealing. "All parents know very young children love to watch other young children; everyone knows children love music; and I think having our characters say and do things that are familiar to the child are essential."[17]

After producing the video in 1988, she ran into a roadblock. Sheryl's video was a hit, and Barney captured the imagination of kids who saw the purple dinosaur. She didn't have enough money to hire an ad agency, though, and with no contacts in the industry, she couldn't get it into distribution. Instead, she recruited a group of moms to help her create a grassroots marketing campaign to promote Barney and the video.

The "Mom Blitzers" started selling the video by cold-calling toy and video stores in a selected area. To sweeten the deal, they offered to buy back any copies the store couldn't sell. Once a few stores were on board, the "Mom Blitzers" sent free copies of the Barney video to preschools and daycare centers in that area. When the kids saw Barney at daycare, they were hooked. To close the loop, Sheryl's team then sent the daycare centers a list of stores where Barney videos were sold locally. She also enlisted retail stores to help pitch Barney to their video distributors. Like John Johnson did with his campaign to build demand at the news-stands, Sheryl got retail stores to help build demand for Barney in the wholesale channel.[18] Sheryl's commonsense approach literally created demand from the ground up.

In 1991, Larry Rifkin rented a Barney video from a Connecticut video store for 4-year-old Leora. Larry happened to be the executive vice president of programming for Connecticut Public Television, and when he saw how captivated his daughter was with the video, he called Sheryl and offered to put Barney on public television. *Barney & Friends* made its debut on the Public Broadcasting Service (PBS) in April 1992 and quickly became the number-one preschool show.[19] Hasbro rolled out 20 licensed Barney toys, including a talking dinosaur that recited 572 phrases, and EMI Records released a Barney music album. Within a year of its debut on PBS, Barney catapulted past *Sesame Street* to become the number-one preschool show, and parents bought more than $300 million worth of Barney items—not counting sleepwear, linens, and lunch boxes.[20]

By creating their own demand, Sheryl and her "Mom Blitzers" built Barney into a runaway success. Lyrick sold 65 million Barney home videos and more than 100 million Barney books, including several best-sellers. Ten years later, an estimated 97 percent of U.S. households had at least one Barney product, and "A Day in the Park with Barney" be-came a permanent attraction at the Universal Studios theme park in Florida.[21] In 2001, HIT Entertainment, owner of *Bob the Builder*, another popular children's show, acquired Lyrick for $275 million.[22]

Pounding the Pavement

While publicity stunts and generating your own demand can help cre-ate buzz, there's no replacing good old-fashioned selling. Shortly after starting Boston Beer Company, Jim Koch got a call from his uncle, a partner at Goldman Sachs, who was also one of his early investors. Jim explained that the first batch of Samuel Adams beer was aging in the tanks and would be ready to deliver in a few weeks.

"So what did you do today?" his uncle asked. Jim explained that he had spent the day shopping for a computer so he could keep track of his sales and accounting information.

"Oh yeah, sales," he said. "Have you got any?" Jim admitted that he hadn't. "So what the hell are you doing buying a computer?" his uncle demanded. "I've seen a lot more businesses go broke because they didn't have enough sales than I've seen go under from lack of computers. Why don't you work on first things first?"[23]

His uncle's wake-up call shook him up. Jim realized with alarm that he didn't need a computer or an accounting system or even an office. What he really needed were customers. From that point on, he gave himself a quota of landing one new account a day. Armed with a new attitude and a briefcase full of beer, Jim visited local bars and restaurants around the city, making friends and dropping off samples.[24]

After pounding the pavement and talking to bartenders all over town, Jim increased his customer base to 30 accounts. He continued with his self-imposed quota and got it up to 60 accounts. He visited each new account regularly, cementing the relationship and angling for a bigger share of their business. He couldn't afford fancy marketing materials, so Jim created an inexpensive black-and-white table tent that said, "Drink Sam Adams." They weren't particularly attractive, but he trekked around the city visiting bars and taverns that were already selling Samuel Adams, asking, "You don't mind if I put these on the tables, do you?" Most agreed and let him put out the homemade ads. When customers walked into the bar, the first thing they saw was the Sam Adams table tent.[25]

In his prospectus to potential investors before starting the company, Jim estimated that the company would have to sell 5,000 barrels a year to reach profitability, projected in three to five years. He was way off. It took him only eight months to sell the first 5,000 barrels.[26]

As the company grew, Jim continued in his self-appointed role as chief promoter for Sam Adams.[27] "If more CEOs had to go out and sell their products, day in and day out, they'd pay a lot more attention to what they were making," Jim explained. "The more unwilling they are to put themselves in the middle of that transaction, the better chance they have of missing out on a critical element of their business. When you're out there selling, face-to-face with your customer, there's no place to hide. It's the acid test."[28]

One Customer at a Time

Emma Chappell learned the same lesson in the banking industry. After coming up through the ranks to become vice president of Continental Bank, Emma was the first African-American woman to serve as an officer of a national bank. She didn't think the major banks were doing a good job lending to underserved neighborhoods, and she believed she could make a bigger contribution by starting a new bank that focused on neighborhoods others overlooked. She quit her job, lived on savings—while still supporting two daughters—and began lining up support to start a new bank.[29]

Her initial plan was to approach big financial institutions as investors. When the stock market crashed in 1987, institutional investors vanished and she had to change her game plan. Instead of signing up big investors, she went door-to-door, personally selling stock at $10 a share in blocks of 50 shares, for a minimum investment of $500. Responding to her tireless campaign, nearly 3,000 African-Americans and others purchased her stock and she raised the $3 million required by the state of Pennsylvania. When she went to Harrisburg to register the bank, though, state officials told her they had raised the minimum to $5 million. "That is when my heart really sunk," Emma said. "They never gave a reason, other than to say it was a different economy, so you need more money to start."[30]

While others may have given up, Emma dug in her heels and continued her tireless campaign looking for investors. She canvassed different neighborhoods in Philadelphia, shaking hands with blue-collar workers, entrepreneurs, and professionals—telling anyone who would listen about her new bank. She also continued working to push major corporations, and enlisted help from city hall. Then she had an inspiration—the best place to spread her gospel was in churches. She talked local ministers into letting her address their congregations, which raised the economic consciousness of the African-American community. It took her another year, but Emma raised $6 million—$1 million more than the regulators required—and officially opened the bank's doors.[31]

When the U.S. Treasury established the Community Development Financial Institutions Program, Emma received certification for a nonprofit called Philadelphia United. To help entrepreneurs start and grow their businesses, Philadelphia United began offering education and training programs for small businesses, management classes, and help with writing business plans. It also created a $2 million low-interest loan fund. The bank created 80 jobs directly and 4,000 to 5,000 jobs indirectly.[32]

"My mission has been to maintain banking services in these underserved neighborhoods, which then allows for the economic viability of those neighborhoods," Emma said. United Bank of Philadelphia also acquired six more branches—failed savings and loans in other minority neighborhoods in Philadelphia—from the Resolution Trust Corp.[33]

Creative Ways to Spread the Word

You don't need a Madison Avenue ad agency if you're willing to work hard and think creatively. When he couldn't get distributors to carry his new magazine, John Johnson recruited friends to create demand at Chicago newsstands, putting the wheels in motion to build a publishing empire. Sheryl Leach used a similar idea to promote her Barney video, demonstrating that somebody with no industry experience, operating on her own instincts with common sense as her guide, could transform a new idea into a huge success.

Although he wasn't as outrageous as Nick Graham or Richard Branson, Stelios Haji-Ionnou built a reputation for creatively breaking the rules and getting a lot of free publicity in the process. Like Stelios flying on his competitor's maiden flight, Chris Emery and Larry Finnson took over the Dairy Queen auction, and got the access they wanted and plenty of free publicity in the process. Neither Dave Gold (99 Cents Only) nor Richard Tait and Whit Alexander (Cranium) had money for a big ad campaign, but both used ingenuity and creativity to get their message out in the media.

In each case, entrepreneurs who didn't have a big advertising budget used creativity, drive, and determination to promote their companies. Although it took her six years to get it off the ground, United Bank of Philadelphia came into existence because Emma Chappell was unwilling to take no for an answer and she took her campaign to the streets. Emma proved that good old-fashioned pounding the pavement could open a lot of doors—if you have patience, persistence, and a belief in your product.

Chapter 9

Find Out What Your Customers *Really* Want

In the early days of Cisco Systems, CEO John Morgridge instilled a relentless customer focus; not out of any sense of enlightened management, but for purely practical reasons. The company simply couldn't afford to build something that customers might not want. Instead of guessing what customers wanted, they asked them first. That's the same principle that propelled Dell to the top of the computer industry. As a young entrepreneur, Michael Dell couldn't afford to stock inventory like his bigger competitors. His solution was build-to-order computers, so he could buy the parts after he knew the customer wanted the computer. The problem is that the more successful a company is, the further away the decision-makers get from the actual customers, and that distance makes it difficult to determine the needs of the consumers.

This sounds obvious, but plenty of smart people at successful companies get into trouble because of it. They think they know what customers want, and they spend huge amounts of time, money, and resources trying to provide it. Their biggest mistake isn't that they miss the target, but that they're shooting at the wrong target. The things that are important to you might not be important to your customers. If you don't stop to find out what your customers *really* want, you're in danger of making products customers aren't interested in.

Listen to Your Customers

Even if you don't have a built-to-order business model, there are some pretty simple ways to find out what your customers really want. When John McAdam was running the European sales division of Sequent Computers Systems, he grew the division from $8 million to $300 million in three years before being promoted to President and COO. A large part of his success was the result of frequent input from his customers. Unlike consumers who can't necessarily envision a new product before they've seen it, John was selling high-end computer systems to sophisticated customers who knew exactly what was coming down the road in the industry.

Instead of simply commissioning a survey, or even meeting with customers one-on-one (both of which he did), John took it a step further. Sequent held architectural council meetings with customers twice a year, gathering some of their biggest and some of their smallest customers together for three days off site. Instead of just the marketing, sales, and senior executives representing the company, Sequent also had front-line engineers and product development people participate in the customer meetings.

Customers loved it because they got to talk directly with the people who were actually building the products. They also got a good idea what was going on in the product road map, and they had the opportunity to influence the outcome with their suggestions. On the flip side, the engineers got firsthand feedback from customers who were actually using what they built. In addition to getting the engineers charged up and motivated, it also gave them invaluable feedback that helped them improve the products.

The event would kick off Thursday night, which was largely socializing over drinks and dinner to break the ice. They held meetings all day Friday in small groups. Friday night was another round of socializing, and by Saturday morning they were hearing *exactly* what the customers thought. "I don't know what it is about a weekend, but it was amazing the feedback we'd get on a Saturday morning from the customers," John explains. "It takes about 24 hours of interaction before they get there. When we meet them on a Thursday it's a customer-supplier relationship. There's some of that during the day on the Friday, and it just seems to become more of a trusting relationship over time."[1]

The customer input went far beyond just improving existing products; it led the company in an entirely new direction. "We changed product strategy based on it," John said. "One of the things that I learned about it was how deep the knowledge customers have got about the industry. I know that sounds stupid, but suppliers tend to take it for granted that they know everything. We would get unbelievable feedback from customers. Stuff like that, there's just no way you could get it within your own company." IBM later bought Sequent for $810 million. Based on his success at Sequent, John introduced the same program later when he became CEO of F5 Networks. By working directly with customers, F5's front-line managers and engineers both walked away better equipped to help solve their customers' problems.

Find Their Hot Button

Sales and business development people often get so focused on their pitch that they don't stop to find out what's really important to the customer. The benefits in your PowerPoint slides are all fine and dandy, but if your customers want something else, they couldn't care less. When Norm Brodsky started Perfect Courier, there were 300 to 400 messenger companies in Manhattan, and competition was tough. Norm quickly discovered the only way he could land new customers was by offering lower prices, but it would be tough to survive in business that way. The turning point came when the office manager at a law firm told him that what she really wanted wasn't cheaper service, but better invoices. At that time, courier companies would list all the pickups and deliveries together on one invoice, and it was a time-consuming task to assign those charges to the appropriate client. The office manager said she'd give all her business to any messenger company that could give her invoices itemized by client.[2]

Armed with a new angle and hot prospect, he found a computer programmer, redesigned the invoices, and landed the account. The new billing system became Perfect Courier's competitive advantage, and, for a while, it was the one thing they could offer that their competitors couldn't answer. His competitors eventually caught on and followed suit, but not until Perfect Courier carved out a solid client list. Perfect Courier was on the *Inc.* 500 list of the fastest growing public companies three years in a row, and after merging with CitiPostal, it was on the *Inc.* 100 list of fastest growing public companies.[3]

The *New York Times* learned the same exact lesson 25 years later, when it was pushing hard to expand beyond its regional base in the Northeast. The problem was that the paper was difficult to find in many places outside the Northeast, and customers didn't know where to look for it. With more than 2,700 Starbucks stores across the country, an alliance with Starbucks made perfect sense. Starbucks, on the other hand, had its own reasons for wanting to sell newspapers. Customers were more inclined to linger over a newspaper, spending more time in the store, and, hopefully, spending more money. The opportunity was pretty clear, but the decision had already been made years earlier—Starbucks was selling *USA Today* in its stores.[4]

Although the demographics of the *New York Times* closely matched that of Starbucks customers, *USA Today* also had good coverage. Furthermore, *USA Today* costs less, and the name might be more appealing to customers in Des Moine or San Diego. What tipped the scales was Norm Brodsky's secret weapon—billing. The *New York Times* was able clinch the deal by promising something *USA Today* was unable to provide—one centralized bill for all Starbucks stores nationwide. To deliver on this promise, the *New York Times* had a team of programmers work around the clock to write the code, but they got it done and they won the account.[5] If you can find their hot button, you can solve your customers' problem and you both come out ahead. Sometimes the competitive edge you're looking for is right in front of you, but you won't even know it unless you ask.

The 47th Mover Advantage

Scott Cook got the inspiration for Intuit while his wife was balancing the checkbook at their kitchen table. Listening to her complain about paying the bills gave him a flash of insight—paying bills would be a great use of computers. His idea wasn't unique, though, because there were a host of other personal finance products on the market at the time.[6]

His second insight was what made Intuit stand out from the crowd. As an alumni of Procter & Gamble, he learned the lesson well about listening to customers. From the beginning, Scott was obsessed with talking to customers and getting their reaction and feedback firsthand. He got out the phone book and started cold-calling people in Palo Alto, California, and Winnetka, Illinois, both affluent neighborhoods where he figured people were more likely to own a computer. What he confirmed in his phone interviews was that most people disliked managing their finances, and, in particular, balancing their checkbooks.[7] Scott teamed up with Tom Proulx, a Stanford undergrad who was a computer programmer, and they began working on their own personal finance program.

At the time, the number-one financial software program on the market was Andrew Tobias's *Managing Your Money*, which was loaded with features and functionality, including portfolio analysis and financial modeling. There was a prevailing opinion in the computer industry—then and now— that the more features you had, the more your customers would like it. Scott was convinced this common belief was wrong. In talking to potential customers, he realized that they weren't excited by all the bells and whistles. They just wanted something to get the job done quickly and easily.

Instead of competing with other financial programs on features, Intuit took a completely different approach, focusing entirely on making it easy to write checks and balance your checkbook. It made its software interface look like a checkbook so people could intuitively understand how to use it (hence the name Intuit). By making it easy, Intuit was able to dominate a market segment with a program that had far fewer features and capabilities than other software on the market.[8] But it was easy to use, and that's what customers wanted. "We made Quicken fast and easy," Scott said. "The catch is, if you're going to make it fast and easy, it's got to be fast and easy in the hands of the customer, not in my hands or an engineer's hands."[9]

For Intuit's first usability study, it recruited novices from the Palo Alto Junior League who knew nothing about computers. Scott and Tom reasoned that if these computer novices couldn't get the program up and running, and figure out how to print a check in 15 minutes, it was too complicated. The Junior Leaguers did fine filling out the check outlines on their computer screens, but they had trouble getting the printed checks lined up right. The two entrepreneurs cringed. "We knew one thing," Tom recalled. "If people had that much trouble the first time they used the program, they'd never use it again."[10]

As the company grew, Scott's fixation on the customer continued. Taking a page out of the P&G marketing book, he implemented "follow me home research." Intuit employees actually followed customers home from the retail store—with their permission, of course—to watch them install Quicken in their home. "You watch their eyebrows, where they hesitate, where they have a quizzical look," said Cook. "Every glitch, every momentary hesitation is our fault."[11] Watching customers firsthand was a powerful lesson that taught engineers and marketers the lesson of what they needed to improve.[12]

Regardless of their position, everyone in the company worked the customer support phones on a regular basis. Scott and his cofounder, Tom Proulx, were right there taking calls themselves. Whether customers were calling with complaints or suggestions, everyone got direct, unfiltered feedback. This practice created a strong customer-centric culture that kept them focused on what really mattered. Intuit also developed a database to track customer feedback, with the results distributed throughout the company. Managers called customers from their product registration cards, asking for feedback and suggestions on improving Quicken. They even listened to tapes of customer service calls while they drove to work.[13]

The goal wasn't just to help customers solve their problems today; it was to find out where customers were having trouble so they could make Quicken better. The engineers, who are usually at an arm's length from customers, saw exactly where customers fumbled with the program, giving them a feedback loop that let them continually improve the product. Everyone at Intuit embraced Scott's belief that they needed to figure out what customers wanted and drive the company to deliver it. "If you blow that," Scott argued, "it doesn't matter what else you do.[14]

At the outset, Scott Cook and Tom Proulx analyzed the other 46 competing products on the market, joking that they had the 47th mover advantage.[15] By talking to potential customers and watching them use their product firsthand, they found the one key that all their competitors missed. Customers didn't want a program loaded with more features, they wanted something that was easy to use. Although they had their share of bumps along the way, Scott and Tom built Intuit into the industry leader, and Quicken forever changed the landscape of the software industry. Although they didn't know it at the time, Intuit's relentless focus on the customer became a key weapon in the company's survival when Microsoft made a direct assault on Quicken later.

Follow the Money

Most people assume that PayPal's online payment system was successful only because of the growth in eBay auctions. In fact, eBay had its own payment service, Billpoint, and it went to great lengths to steer customers to its own solution. To help speed adoption of Billpoint, eBay brought in Wells Fargo as an equity investor and signed a strategic partnership agreement with Visa. EBay strongly promoted Billpoint to its customers, including giving credits toward listing fees to customers who sold items using Billpoint. EBay later introduced a controversial checkout feature, strongly encouraging customers to use Billpoint for payments.[16]

EBay's fatal flaw was limiting Billpoint payments to transactions on eBay. Many people had auctions on eBay, Amazon, and Yahoo. Customers could use PayPal for all their auctions, but Billpoint only worked on eBay. By trying to lock their customers in, eBay bred resentment among its customers.

Despite stiff resistance from eBay, PayPal continued to thrive for one reason—customers liked it better. It was easier to use and they could make payments anywhere they liked. Customers voted with their wallets, choosing PayPal over Billpoint by a wide margin. To eBay's credit, it eventually read the handwriting on the wall, and acquired PayPal for $1.5 billion and quietly shut down Billpoint. By focusing on its strategy and not its customers, eBay got trounced on it's own turf.

Blinded by Success

Finding out what's important to your customers is just as important for established companies as it is for start-ups. For the first decade cellular phones were commercially available, Motorola virtually owned the cellular industry. Known for building rugged, durable handsets, Motorola blew past the competition when it introduced the flip phone, the first portable phone that was small enough to easily fit into a shirt pocket or purse. As it introduced newer models, Motorola made sure new models were compatible with older accessories, making it cheaper and easier to keep its customers loyal. As success built on success, Motorola got further and further away from its customers. The company's past success became a stumbling block when Motorola executives were convinced that they knew more about what customers wanted than their customers did.

Not only did Motorola executives fail to anticipate the demand for digital phones, they completely ignored—and even dismissed—repeated demands for digital from their customers. Because digital wireless networks let wireless carriers add three to six times as many customers using the same frequency as analog, cellular carriers had a huge incentive to upgrade. This increase in capacity would translate into lower costs for the carriers and lower prices for the customers. Digital phones also offered customers new features such as Caller ID and voice-mail notification, which were not available in analog phones. The downside was that digital phones were larger, because they had to squeeze both digital and analog circuit boards into the same handset.

Despite a huge campaign by wireless carriers to entice customers to upgrade to digital, Motorola continued pushing smaller analog models.[17] By doggedly sticking to their goal of making phones smaller, they ignored and dismissed repeated demands from their customers—the cellular carriers. Like Microsoft engineers loading the program Money with features, Motorola was too focused on what its engineers wanted to build and not what its customers wanted to buy.

The result was entirely predictable. Nimble competitors such as Nokia and Samsung quickly stepped in to meet the growing demand for digital phones and their sales soared. Motorola's continued denial of the move toward digital made its fortunes go from bad to worse. Motorola's market share plunged from 60 percent in the early 1990s to 14 percent by 2001.[18] Although it finally embraced digital handsets in 1998, the damage was already done, and it abdicated its leadership position in the marketplace.[19] The company that virtually owned the cellular industry at the beginning of the decade found itself battling for third place. Motorola wasn't derailed by poor-quality products, and it still had leaders with vision, great engineers, and a lot of very smart people working very hard. It just wasn't making what customers wanted to buy.

Same Problem, Different Industry

Several years after Motorola's fall from grace, Intel nearly made the same mistake by focusing on technology the engineers liked instead of what customers really wanted. Like Motorola, Intel was an engineering-centric company that rose to become the leader in its industry. For years, Intel's efforts focused on making chips faster and adding more features. In doing so, both the software and hardware makers benefited. When a new version of Windows came out, the new operating systems were so big customers needed to upgrade their hardware to run them. After a while, though, the incremental gains in speed weren't enough to drive new PC sales, and Intel's sales stalled. Furthermore, the faster chips caused laptops to heat up, and adding features raised the price, even if customers didn't want those features.

When Paul Otellini became president and chief operating officer of Intel, he was the first nonengineer to ascend to the top of the chip-making powerhouse. Unlike his predecessors, Paul came up through the ranks on the marketing side of the company. With his different background he also brought in a different perspective, and he put his marketing background to work by focusing on customers instead of technology.

Instead of focusing on ever-faster clock speeds, Paul pushed Intel to listen to what customers actually want and to develop products accordingly. As he explains it, being a product guy instead of an engineer allows him to ask "higher level dumb questions." In talking to customers, he realized that customers didn't really care if the processor was 2.4 GHz or 2.6 GHz. They wanted smaller laptops and Wi-Fi wireless technology, which drained the battery faster. For the first time, speed wasn't important to customers anymore. What they did want was longer battery life on laptops.

To change the ingrained corporate culture of focusing on clock speed above all else, Paul brought independent teams together to collaborate for the first time. In a huge departure from past tradition, Paul pushed engineers to move in a new direction. Continuing to focus on making chips even faster would have been tantamount to Motorola's single-minded goal of making analog phones smaller and ignoring digital.[20]

In the spring of 2001, engineers from Intel's office in Israel pitched senior management on a radical new plan. Instead of starting with a desktop microprocessor and modifying it for laptops, the Israeli team wanted to build a new system from the ground up to improve battery life. With Paul backing them, the Israeli team redesigned a new microprocessor with a much longer battery life, then collaborated with other Intel teams working on Wi-Fi chipsets. Their new Pentium M used less than a third of the power of earlier chips, and it performed many functions faster than earlier chips with higher clock speeds. It was also about two-thirds the size, making it cheaper to manufacture.[21]

Instead of continuing down the same path and building what engineers wanted, Intel retooled and focused on building what customers were asking for. Battery life took precedence over clock speed, and features weren't added unless customers actually wanted them. "We do not put a feature into a microprocessor anymore unless we know how we will market it and what the end-user benefits will be," Paul said. "That is 180 degrees different from the 'build a better mousetrap and the world will beat a path to our door' model that we had for a long time."[22]

To appeal to customers with different needs, Intel introduced several flavors of Pentium M, including low-voltage and ultra low-voltage models. Intel also launched the Centrino, a bundle that includes Pentium M processor and a wireless chipset.[23] Paul's strategy paid off in a big way as Intel's Centrino chips got off to a strong start, selling 2 million Centrino chips per quarter.[24] Intel is still a world-class engineering company. But by listening to customers—instead of engineers—it avoided Motorola's mistake and remained at the pinnacle of the industry.

Do They Want What You Think They Want?

Finding out what customers want sounds so elementary that the question is often dismissed out of hand. *Of course we know what our customers want.*

But unless you ask them, you may be making dangerous assumptions. The danger is that they may not want what you think they want. If you guess wrong, you may be running 100 miles an hour in the wrong direction.

Motorola was convinced that customers cared more about a smaller sized phone than one that is digital. That miscalculation nearly derailed the company, and Motorola lost its leadership position in the industry. Similarly, Intel engineers were convinced that customers wanted faster processors and more features. Of course, that's something tangible an engineer can really appreciate. But until Paul Otellini redirected them, they were in danger of making the same mistake as Motorola.

Customers are buying the benefits, not the features. They don't want more bells and whistles. They want you to solve their problem. By talking to customers, Scott Cook at Intuit realized that people didn't want more features in their personal finance program, they wanted it to be easier. By focusing on one simple thing—printing a check easily—Scott reshaped the entire industry. Norm Brodsky learned the same thing at Perfect Courier when he discovered that his customers wanted better invoices, not lower prices. Find out what your customers really want—before you make it—and you'll have a real competitive advantage.

"You'd better understand what your customers' needs are if you want to meet or exceed their expectations," said venture capital veteran and former Macy's CEO Phil Schlein. "Every time I started to make a decision that didn't start with the customer and work back, it's always turned out to be a faulty position."[25]

Chapter 10

Turn Customer Complaints
Into a Secret Weapon

Despite their best intentions, most companies relegate customer service to the bottom of the food chain. Even companies that spend millions on customer relationship management (CRM) software hoping to improve customer relations still have the lowest paid, least experienced people in the company handle most of the customer calls. In many cases, 100 percent of the company's effort is directed at solving the customer's problem so they'll stop calling. The goal, in effect, is to make the complaints go away. If the lowest level reps can't solve a problem, they escalate it up the chain, handing the customer off to somebody more knowledgeable. The problem with this system should be obvious. Customers get frustrated after dealing with several different people, and customer satisfaction goes downhill fast.

In addition to not taking care of the customer properly, there is another hidden danger in this approach. By remaining at arm's length from customer complaints, the decision-makers in any organization are missing an invaluable source of market intelligence. Even if the calls are categorized, counted, and reported up the chain of command, the senior managers are usually so far removed that they get very little useful feedback from these customer complaints. Instead of simply reading the summary reports, you can learn a whole lot more about the problems within your company—and the opportunities to set yourself apart from your competitors—by taking customer support calls yourself on a regular basis. You may hear a little ranting and raving, but you'll also get invaluable market intelligence, competitive updates, and suggestions for improvement. All you have to do is listen.

Turn Customer Support Upside Down

When Wayne Inouye took over eMachines, the company was headed for disaster. The return rate on their PCs was 20 percent, the highest in the industry. The red ink was flowing, and shortly after he arrived, the company was delisted by NASDAQ. He used a different approach than Intuit, but with the same net effect.

Given the dire situation at the company, he immediately went into triage mode. Although eMachines had a bad reputation for quality, the computers actually weren't all that bad. The hardware failure rate from things such as broken drives and damage during shipping was in line with the industry overall. Nonetheless, the customer satisfaction rate was terrible, and with 20 percent of the computers coming back, it was costing a bundle of money. Each computer sent back cost the company about $250. In addition to the actual shipping, somebody needs to deal with it, process it, and figure out what to do with it. And in the end they have a used PC.

Like many other companies, eMachines had the least experienced reps take the initial "tier one" calls. If they couldn't solve the problem, they would transfer it to someone at tier two, and so on. By the time they got to tier four, the most knowledgeable reps, customers were so frustrated by repeating the problem and getting transferred repeatedly that they were ready to give up. Wayne knew from personal experience how frustrating it was to have to call back several times to solve a technical problem. It's also tremendously inefficient to have several people dealing with the same problem.

The first thing he did was turn the whole idea of customer support upside down. Instead of trying to decrease the number of problems, he focused on solving each problem on the first call. To do that, Wayne had top tier technicians handle every call, and the most important thing he measured was first-call resolution.[1] In many cases, it was a software conflict that could be resolved by a knowledgeable support person.

A byproduct of this decision was that the experienced engineers handling the calls were in a position to do something to solve the problems. One thing they quickly realized was that many problems were not with the computer itself, but rather, the free software bundled onto the PC when it was shipped. Known in the computer industry as *shovel-ware*, the practice was to load up PCs with demo versions of different software in return for a commission from the software maker. While it seemed like a harmless practice and a way to make a little extra money on the side, it was actually creating a huge problem. The software wasn't tested for compatibility, and when customers tried removing some of these shovel-ware programs, other things stopped working. Wayne immediately eliminated all the software "extras," a simple fix that greatly reduced the number of customer support calls that had nothing to do with the computer itself.

He did some other things against conventional wisdom. Because customer support costs money, most companies bury the phone number in the manual to discourage calls. The serial number is on the back of the machine where it's hard to read. Wayne responded by putting the serial number and the company's support number on the front of every PC. Instead of trying to discourage customers from calling, he made it easy for them to call. That let him know exactly what the problems were and let him address them before he lost a customer.

When customers did call with hardware problems, tech support engineers had to explain how to remove a faulty drive or power supply so they wouldn't have to send the whole computer back. Even removing the outside cover was a painful proposition. The old machines had several screws that attached the case to the frame, and it was difficult to remove. When a customer did get the case off, the edges were sharp and dangerous. As eMachines designed new models, it kept this in mind. The new eMachines models have two thumbscrews on the side, so the customer can remove the side panel with no tools whatsoever, and the edges are rounded. That simple change made it much easier to open if something did go wrong.

In addition to making it easy to open, eMachines makes it easy for customers to get replacement parts. If something does go wrong with the hardware, the company will send out a replacement part—secured with a credit card to ensure the customer sends the faulty part back. In addition to being cheaper and faster (customers don't have to wait for the computer to be sent in, fixed, and returned), it's also more secure, because they don't have to worry about sending the contents of their hard drive through the mail. In addition to making it easier for the customer, this change also saved the company a substantial amount of money. Three quarters of the customers in the United States who have a problem use this program, and in Japan, where everyone said it would never work, 81 percent of the customers use it.

By redesigning the PCs to minimize problems, and focusing on solving those problems quickly and easily when they do occur, Wayne and his team performed a near miracle. The company that was sliding toward the abyss when he arrived soon became solidly profitable, and eMachines passed Gateway to claim the title of the number-three PC maker in the United States. Equally impressive is the company's customer satisfaction rate. After Wayne took over, eMachines went from the highest return rate in the industry to the lowest.[2]

By changing the way the company handled customer complaints, and listening to those complaints to change both the product and the process in the future, Wayne led a remarkable turnaround at eMachines. "I'm still convinced that brand is created by how you treat customers after they buy a product," Wayne said. "You have to make a good product, but what really sets you apart is how you deal with customers when something does go wrong."

The Buck Starts Here

You don't need an MBA to know that customer service is important. Unfortunately, the buck usually stops there. Dave Duffield took an unusual step from the very beginning at PeopleSoft. To ensure open communication, Dave put his phone number and e-mail address on the last slide at every user conference. "Everyone knew in the company that a customer could call me or a senior VP. We weren't trying to hide anything. I got calls from customers that were very heated. Some were off base, some were right on target. But we just established a very open communication."

By personally taking the call when a customer had a complaint, Dave got unfiltered feedback and he found out in no uncertain terms when there was a problem in the software. Equally as important, he got a lot of suggestions and ideas for future releases. "You learn a lot from them, you get to assimilate a lot of their constructive ideas on what we should be doing in the product or what other product lines might be important," Dave said. "I think it's critical that the leader of the of the organization get to know not every customer, but certainly the key ones, and be involved in the sales situations, because that's where you see what the competition has to offer, where you're missing things, what advantages you have, and getting to formulate your marketing strategies and sales presentations a little bit better."

In addition to going to Users Groups and conferences, Dave made it a point to personally visit some customers who were hot under the collar or upset with the company for one reason or another. By listening to their complaints and addressing the issues head-on—instead of trying to dodge the issue or hand off the complaint to some unlucky subordinate—he often defused the issue while he went back to solve the problem. Equally important, he tapped into a vein of gold by learning firsthand where they had room for improvement.

It's not always bad news, either. One day Dave was invited to the headquarters of Gap, Inc., one of PeopleSoft's early database customers. Because its products were fairly new, he went in prepared for the worst. "I was sitting down with the CIO, the CFO, and all their underlings, expecting someone to yell at me," Dave recalls. "Rather than yelling, they turned around and said they just had to tell me to my face that this has been a great experience, you guys are terrific, and now we want you to consider selling us your HR system."[3]

How Can We Solve the Problem?

When Linksys started selling home networking devices, Janie and Victor Tsao got bad reports back from some retail partners who were selling their products. Because of the complexity of installing a home network, customers would buy various components from different manufacturers only to discover when they got home that the different pieces didn't work together. Even if the components were compatible, many customers realized later that they didn't buy all the parts and pieces needed. The whole process was very confusing and could be extremely frustrating, especially for novice computer users. The natural target for this frustration was the retailer who sold the product. It didn't take long for the word to get out that setting up a home network was a pain in the neck, with retailers taking the brunt of the complaints. When the retailers talked to the vendors, there was a lot of finger-pointing among them, with everyone blaming the problems on somebody else.

In talking with their retail partners, Janie heard these stories about high returns and high customer frustration. In lamenting the problem, one retailer commented that it's too bad nobody puts all this stuff in one box. That complaint led to a new product. Linksys ran with the idea, introducing its "Network in a Box." It contained a network card, a hub, connectors, and cables—everything someone needed to connect two or three computers together. The Network in a Box became a runaway success, and Linksys was widely acclaimed as the first company to make home networking easy.

"Now it seems like a very easy concept, but nobody was doing that," Victor explains. "It wasn't because we were so smart. It was because we were talking to customers. They found that the return rate was high and the customer frustration level was high, and we said, 'How can we solve the problem?' These kinds of things are not rocket science. When you take ownership of the problem and you start brainstorming, these are the things you come up with."[4]

Calling Ben Hill

Using customer complaints to drive future decisions isn't limited to technology companies. Bernie Marcus and Arthur Blank took a novel and somewhat wacky approach to customer service at Home Depot by creating a fictional Vice President of Customer Satisfaction, Ben Hill. They posted signs prominently in every store, complete with a drawing of a man with an orange apron and a Home Depot baseball cap that looked like Pat Farrah, the vice president of merchandising who was a legend among employees in the stores. Each sign had a toll-free number and invited customers to call Ben Hill if they had any problems.[5]

Whenever a customer called Ben Hill with a complaint, it rang directly into the executive suite in Atlanta. Bernie, Arthur, Pat, and any other senior executives who were in the office would answer it. Word got around very quickly among the associates that you don't let a customer leave a Home Depot store unhappy, because if that customer called Ben Hill, the next phone call would be from Bernie or Arthur to the store.[6]

The Ben Hill number not only kept the leaders in touch with the problems in the stores, but also gave the employees a strong incentive to solve customer problems before they got elevated to the big bosses. "Part of Ben Hill's purpose was to create a culture in which you will be personally responsible for the customers in your stores," Bernie explains. "Every time a customer calls Ben Hill, it reflects a failure in the store. But the managers and associates in that store have all the power and all the responsibility in the world to fix any problem that any customer has."[7]

By creating a permanent back-channel line of communication, Bernie and Arthur got feedback much faster and much clearer than they ever could have gotten through a regular reporting system. And there was no chance that a store manager—or anyone else in the chain of command— could sweep problems under the rug to make their department look better. Everybody knew that the two big guys were taking customer calls. If there was a problem, they'd better solve it while it was still in the store. As the company grew and the volume of calls increased, other experienced staffers regularly manned the Ben Hill phone line, including home-improvement experts to answer customer questions about specific projects. The two partners continued to take the calls on a regular basis, though, and they continually reinforced the message to Home Depot associates that the customer comes first.[8]

Because this vital information was going directly to the decision-makers, Bernie, Arthur, and the other senior executives were in a position to act on it. When they got too many complaints from one store about long lines or crowded parking lots, they looked for locations nearby where they could open another store to relieve some of the pressure. When customers complained there weren't enough associates in the store to help them, they tested a new computerized manning system that matched the number of employees to the number of sales from each department. When customers complained about a product being out of stock, they sent employees to buy it from their competitors, knowing it was better to lose money on the sale than lose the customer forever.[9]

They could have had the stores collect customer comments, compile the statistics, and send it up the chain of command. Many other companies do exactly that. But that system would never give Bernie and Arthur the same level of detail they got by talking directly to the customer. "We have customers on a lease, a short lease. Its terms state they will be with us just as long as we take care of them. The longer we take care of them, the longer the lease goes. They will even forgive us a misstep once or twice," Arthur said. "But we can't mess with the lease more than twice. We will lose them. Just like that. They will be gone. And we won't know it until they take their family and friends with them."[10]

The Hidden Intelligence in Customer Support

Instead of viewing customer support as a way to appease callers and hope they don't call back, turn the tables and look at it from the perspective of market intelligence. When customers are complaining, you know exactly what you need to improve. The very same upset customer is giving you valuable information that can help you improve your product, streamline your operation, and make your company more competitive in the future.

But a customer-oriented culture isn't something that happens by decree. It's the result of a message continually demonstrated and constantly reinforced by the leaders in an organization. Home Depot employees knew they'd better solve customers' problems before the customers called Ben Hill and spoke to Bernie or Arthur. Dave Duffield could have directed irate callers to someone else in the company, but he published his phone number and took customer complaints himself.

Don't look at customer complaints as a headache. Look at them as an opportunity. In addition to finding out what the company is doing right, you can hear straight from the customers where you're falling short, what the competition has to offer, and how you stack up in their eyes. Equally important, it sends a message to everybody else downstream that if it's important enough for the boss to get involved, then it's pretty important. There is a wealth of information going untapped. All you have to do is walk down the hall and pick up a headset.

Chapter 11

If You Don't Live in the Present, You Can't Get to the Future

It's easy to get so caught up in your future projections that you don't keep an eye on what you're spending to get there. If you're not careful, expenses can get out of control quickly, and if your revenues come up short, you could be in a world of hurt.

Despite the rosy projections from analysts when most of the telecom industry was caught up in mergers and global alliances, Cincinnati Bell CEO John LaMacchia anticipated the decline of the traditional telephone as the company's main source of revenue. Convinced that the telephone industry would experience slow growth and increasing competition in the future, John created two new divisions—Cincinnati Bell Information Services (CBIS), to provide billing services to wireless carriers, and Matrixx, to provide staffing and technical expertise for toll-free and automated help lines.[1]

Cincinnati Bell later combined CBIS and Matrixx to form Convergys, and spun it off as a separate company in 1998. Convergys went on to become the industry leader in billing and outsourced solutions for telecommunications, cable, and broadband services, with more than $2.3 billion in revenue. By moving in a different direction, John provided a solid return for investors and kept the company financially strong.

"I always tend to discount people's view of the future," John said. "At the end of the day, you have a business to run. If your results are not good and improving, it doesn't really matter what the future is. If you don't live in the present, you don't get to the future."[2]

Big Plans and Big Expenses, but No Customers

Jim McCann got a lesson in how *not* to run a business when an investor group approached him about acquiring 1-800-FLOWERS, a new start-up in Dallas. After growing his chain of 14 flower shops in New York City, Jim knew all too well how important it was to manage his cash and watch the bottom line. When he went to Dallas to meet with executives from the new start-up, he was shocked at the way they were spending money.

The original 1-800-FLOWERS management team had raised more than $20 million in equity and another $15 million in debt, hoping to create a powerhouse in the floral industry. They built a state-of-the-art telemarketing center with million-dollar telephone switches and top-of-the-line computer systems. They bought 700 mahogany workstations and had 120 managers and two Ph.D.s with degrees in training and education on the payroll before they even had a sales staff to train. They hired a hot ad agency and spent a million dollars on a creative campaign before an equally expensive test launch. They even signed up 6,800 florists nationwide to fill their orders.[3]

The only thing the 1-800-FLOWERS team didn't have was customers. The interest on $15 million in debt alone was enough to cripple the new company, and it didn't take long to realize their business model wouldn't support the high fixed costs they had created.[4] Even as he was negotiating to buy the company, Jim was amazed at the free spending ways of the original management team. Every time he went to Dallas to meet them, he flew coach, rented a cheap car, and stayed in a cheap motel. "But the 1-800-FLOWERS boys would pick me up in a fancy car and we'd dine at the best restaurant in town," Jim said. "They were losing a bloody fortune and still enjoying the expense account lifestyle."[5]

After Jim bought 1-800-FLOWERS, he dumped the expensive call center and turned the company around. Having learned a valuable lesson watching the original team burn through their cash, Jim didn't fall into the trap that many companies did during the Internet bubble. By carefully watching his bottom line, he built 1-800-FLOWERS into the industry leader, with more than $500 million in revenues.

Commonsense Budgeting

Shortly after Google's official launch at the height of the Internet boom, cofounders Larry Page and Sergey Brin made a decision that cut against the grain. With all the big players spending hundreds of millions on ad campaigns to build their brands, there was a feeding frenzy going on in advertising. Google hired a branding consultant who recommended they spend $10 million on a brand identity campaign, including full-page ads in the *Wall Street Journal*.

Cindy McCaffrey, an Apple veteran who joined Google as head of marketing, couldn't even get the ad agencies to return her calls—even with $10 million to spend. When she voiced her frustration to Larry and Sergey, she got a surprising response. They questioned the wisdom of an ad campaign to begin with. Why spend all that money in advertising? Why not invest it in the technology? "They said, 'Let's tell the world about Google by building a great product,'" Cindy said. "For two young guys, they showed a remarkable amount of insight."[6]

Even without an ad campaign, traffic on Google continued to grow through word of mouth. With no banner ads, no portal strategy, and nothing to sell, Google was a simple, clean, and remarkably fast search engine. By keeping their powder dry, they also found themselves in an enviable position later when the Internet bubble burst and the tech wreck hit. When other Internet companies were crashing and burning, Google had money in the bank, a solid technology, and their focus never wavered.

Making a Safe BET

When Bob Johnson was vice president of the National Cable TV Association, he realized that no cable TV company provided programming specifically targeting African-Americans. Through his role in the cable industry, he had gotten to know John Malone, CEO of the nation's largest cable provider, Tele-Communications, Inc. (TCI), At age 33, Bob went to John with his business plan and walked away with $500,000 from the TCI founder to launch the first TV channel targeting African-Americans.[7]

In addition to putting his own money into BET (Black Entertainment Television), John put his prestige behind the new channel. John joined the BET board and helped win subscribers through TCI cable systems. "All of a sudden I had a major investor allied with me who was in the same industry," Bob said. "He was my Good Housekeeping Seal of Approval. Every successful person has mentors or a lot of advisors. In my case it was John Malone."[8] Because he had no previous experience as an entrepreneur, Bob asked his new mentor for advice. John said, "Get your revenues up and keep your costs down."[9]

"BET is really an extension of what John Johnson did with *Ebony* magazine," according to Bob (who is not related to the *Ebony* founder). "No one was talking about this population that wanted to read stories about its successes and accomplishments. BET is a magazine with moving pictures. It's not a new idea to target African-Americans—newspapers had been doing that forever—but it mirrored the technology of the time, satellite and cable."[10]

A year after Bob made his investment into BET, it began airing for two hours on Friday and Saturday nights. Critics questioned his decision to use reruns as part of the content, but given the millions of dollars movie studios spend to keep an audience entertained, Bob knew trying to create all original content would have bankrupted him quickly. "I kept my programming expenses low by broadcasting reruns of black sitcoms such as *The Jeffersons* and music videos of black recording artists." When critics said the programming could be better—even though both Ted Turner and MTV did the exact same thing to keep programming costs down—he pointed out the economics of running a network. "I didn't see the connection between huge expenses in programming and advertisers stepping up their ad rates," Bob said. "They were only going to pay so much."[11]

Instead of blowing his budget, Bob took a careful and pragmatic approach to running the business, balancing his checkbook and following John Malone's advice of "Get your revenues up and keep your costs down." When he realized that nobody was making movies showing the middle-class African-American experience, Bob decided to acquire Arabesque, a publisher of black paperback romance novels. In addition to giving his customers the information and entertainment they wanted, he also secured an inexpensive source of additional content for his target audience.[12] Once again following his mentor's advice, Bob waited to launch the film production unit until BET had critical mass needed to make the investment a safe bet.

His conservative approach to spending paid off and the network grew dramatically over the next two decades. By keeping his revenue up and his costs down, Bob built BET into a media powerhouse reaching more than 62 million households, including three 24-hour cable channels, 2 XM satellite radio channels, Arabesque books, and BET Pictures II, which makes movies and documentaries for BET networks. When Viacom acquired BET in 2001 for $2.5 billion, Bob's stake netted him $1.5 billon in Viacom stock.[13] "Some people think I've tried to do business on the cheap," Bob said, "but too many businesses run into trouble because they don't keep costs in line with revenue."[14]

You Have to Keep the Lights On

Pixar Animations Studios is known to kids throughout the world for creating hits such as *Toy Story* and *Finding Nemo*. Pixar seemed to burst on the scene in 1995 with the world's first fully animated feature. In reality, Pixar's overnight success was anything but. In fact, the company's first decade in business was so tough they had to put their dreams on hold and focus on finding ways to keep the company alive.

Pixar was born in 1986 when Steve Jobs bought the computer graphics assets from George Lucas's film company for $10 million. It started out as an independent lab with the goal of making animated cartoons and movies. Pixar produced several award-winning animated short films, but the high cost of sophisticated computing equipment and the slow production schedule added up and the bills mounted.

Many of the tools they needed simply didn't exist, so the engineers at Pixar invented them along the way. This practice was great from a creative standpoint, but not very practical when you're trying to make money and stay on schedule. Steve later admitted that if he had known how much it would cost to keep Pixar going, he probably never would have bought it. "The problem was, for many years the cost of the computers required to make animation we could sell was tremendously high," he said.[15]

Because the company had built most of its own animation tools, Pixar raised cash by selling its animation software, Renderman. It also made money by creating a new system to help Disney artists streamline their animation process and improve their special effects. Selling software helped address the cash crunch, but it wasn't enough to cover the bills.

To close the gap, Pixar produced animated commercials for Tropicana, Listerine, Trident, The California Lottery, Volkswagen, and Pillsbury. In addition to providing much needed revenue, these commercials helped the team at Pixar refine their tools and improve their animation techniques.

In 1991, Pixar approached Disney to pitch an hour-long animated TV special. By the time Steve Jobs and Michael Eisner finished negotiating, they agreed to a three-movie deal. Production on the first movie took four years to complete, and even with Disney picking up half the tab, Pixar still had significant expenses. Continuing to balance the practical requirements of running a business with the dream of creating animated movies, Pixar produced 29 more commercials and continued refining their development tools.

When *Toy Story* was finally released on Thanksgiving weekend in 1995, it was an immediate hit. Not only was it the first fully computer animated feature film in history, but it was also the highest grossing film all year.[16] Since then, Pixar has had a string of hits with *A Bug's Life*, *Toy Story 2*, *Monsters Inc.*, and *Finding Nemo*. Pixar's first four full-length films grossed $1.5 billion worldwide, in addition to winning 15 Academy Awards.[17] None of that would have happened if Pixar hadn't survived that first tough decade—even though it meant putting the dream on hold temporarily so it could make enough money to keep the doors open.

Stay Flexible and Adapt

When Jeanette White decided to start her own company, she had a strong technical background and she knew there was a big market for the data analysis and systems integration work she could provide. Like many other new entrepreneurs, though, she quickly discovered how hard it was to get her foot in the proverbial door. Because Sytel was a start-up without a strong track record, she had trouble landing clients.

When the consulting contracts she was hoping for didn't materialize, she started offering computer-training classes simply as a matter of expediency. Simply put, the money was trickling in and she had bills to pay. To balance the budget, she ran classes and developed course curricula for desktop applications such as Microsoft Word and Excel, and Oracle databases. "The barrier to entry training was very low and we needed the cash flow it generated to keep us going," Jeanette explained. "We used that as a tactic, not a strategy."[18]

When she started the company, she expected to start taking a salary in about six months. As it turned out, she funded the company on credit cards and she didn't take a paycheck for four and a half years. Whenever the company made some money, she had to choose between taking a paycheck and reinvesting it to grow the business.

Profits from the computer training work allowed Jeanette to hire more engineers and steer the company toward what she saw as a giant hole in the market—systems integration for government agencies. Over time, Sytel developed a reputation for making disparate systems and technologies work together efficiently, and she was able to win larger integration engagements. She landed clients such as the National Institutes of Health, the Department of Agriculture, and the Federal Emergency Management Agency.[19]

She remained opportunistic, looking to see what other offerings she could develop over time. As the federal IT market changed, one new opportunity that emerged was in the area of eGovernment. Sytel got in on the ground floor, developing a skill set in that niche, building on its core competency of network and system integration.

By adapting and evolving with the market, Jeanette built Sytel into a $40 million company and a leading solutions providers in the mid-Atlantic region. She was named Maryland's High Tech Council's executive of the year, she received the national entrepreneur award from *Working Woman* magazine, and Sytel was on the *Inc.* 500 list of the fastest growing companies several times. While Jeannette stayed within her core competency of systems integration, she had enough flexibility to adapt to the changes in the market, looking for targets of opportunity while she bootstrapped her way to success.

Balance the Budget

No matter how great your vision of the future is, you still have to survive long enough to get there. The business landscape is littered with carcasses of companies that had pie-in-the-sky estimates of their industry, but couldn't hold on long enough to see their vision come true. When you're focused on the horizon and not watching the road ahead, it's easy to wind up deep in the woods.

Jeanette White made the same decision as Pixar when she was trying to get Sytel off the ground. When she had trouble landing clients to do computer systems integration work, she offered computer-training classes to augment her ailing revenue stream. The additional cash flow let her stay in business and hire more engineers, providing the same lifeline that commercials offered Pixar.

When companies of all sizes were spending millions on brand campaigns, Larry and Sergey canceled their ad campaign and focused on making Google better and faster—and better—and faster. When you're spending money, don't let ambition overcome good judgment. It doesn't matter how exciting the future is if you're not around to see it.

Chapter 12

If You Choose Profits Over People, You Won't Have Either

Today's business world has become so focused on short-term profits that the formula for success often seems to ignore anything beyond the next quarter. Leaders of public companies are measured not by how well the company is doing, but how well the company is doing *right now*. With 24-hour financial channels dissecting a company's every move, it's easy to ignore the long-term impact of decisions in favor of what will happen next week. The unfortunate side effect is that managers who make decisions with an eye on the stock price are bound to pay for it in spades in the long run.

The two quickest ways to boost short-term earnings in most companies are to cut research and development and cut employees, either by reducing headcount or benefits—or both. When companies announce job cuts, the stock usually goes up. After all, lower employee costs translate into higher profits. Employees and customers aren't the ones cheering, though, as layoffs have a huge impact on the human side of the company. Layoffs not only hurt morale, but they also tend to degrade customer service. If the survival of the company is in jeopardy, layoffs may be unavoidable. But if the only goal is to boost the short-term outlook to keep investors happy today, the long-term economic impact can be devastating for the company.

That's not to say tough measures aren't sometimes necessary. Nissan could not have stayed in business much longer if Carlos Ghosn hadn't implemented his painful and controversial Nissan Turnaround Plan. When Dale Fuller took over Borland, the company was teetering on the edge of bankruptcy, and he wound up firing 60 top managers who couldn't—or wouldn't—get on board with his plan to save the company. So yes, the long-term health and viability of the company may call for layoffs or cuts to keep the company afloat. But all too often executives undertake slash-and-burn tactics for the wrong reasons, and they're counterproductive in the long run.

When Bill George was CEO of Medtronic, he felt pulled in two directions every day. On one hand, doctors wanted more money for research and development of new products. On the other, short-term investors demanded immediate profits. "In the end we based our decisions on what was best for patients. It was the right thing to do, but often a difficult and lonely course to take."[1]

It doesn't take long to realize that the companies that have been consistent winners over the long haul are those that respect and value their employees. That's not just a paragraph in the employee manual or some meaningless assertion by the human resources department. It's part of the company's culture, and it shows from the top down. Those companies focused only on "growing shareholder value" and maximizing the bottom line shouldn't be surprised to find themselves with workforces that are bitter, cynical, and skeptical. "Chainsaw Al" Dunlap, former CEO of Sunbeam, was famous for slashing benefits and cutting thousands of jobs. The "Chainsaw Al" approach may improve the bottom line temporarily, but the damage to the human factor is incalculable.

"You have to get trust within an organization and if they don't trust the leader to operate in the interest of the employee as well as the stockholders, I think you're going to suffer," former Harley-Davidson CEO Rich Teerlink points out.[2] Taking care of your people—both your employees and your customers—can go a long way toward taking care of the company.

Short-Term Profits vs. Long-Term Value

Bernie Marcus and Arthur Blank were legendary at Home Depot for relentlessly instilling a culture of focus on the customer. They also went to great lengths to sidestep the barriers to communication most companies encounter. It was not uncommon for employees to find Bernie or Arthur—or sometimes both of them together—showing up unannounced at all hours to walk through a store to see what was going on. These "store walks" were unscheduled and unscripted. Like David Neeleman at JetBlue, Bernie and Arthur got direct feedback from employees on the front lines, grabbing whoever was nearby and taking them to the break room to chat about the store. In the process, they listened to employees, hearing complaints and suggestions. Equally important was the effect on the people in the stores. Not only did they want to keep everything looking good because the big bosses might show up at any moment, but these visits reinforced the message that what they were doing was important.

Bernie and Arthur went to great lengths to preach that customers were number one; they also made it clear that their employees were a close second. It was all about the people. As Arthur explained it, "Our role is to set the programs, visualize the future, to listen carefully, to train and teach, and then allow these people to do their own thing."[3]

In addition to continually reinforcing the culture of focus on the customer, Home Depot also used smart hiring practices. They hired plumbers to work in the plumbing section and carpenters to work in lumber, so customers with questions had experts on hand to give advice. Anyone who needed advice on what type of wood to use for a deck or what kind of wiring to use for a specific electrical fixture knew Home Depot was the place to go. In addition to a huge selection and low prices, they had experts there to help you. "Payroll is not an expense to us," Arthur said. "It's an investment."[4]

Bernie and Arthur's relentless focus on the customer was a key factor in Home Depot's phenomenal success. But think about what would have happened if they had chosen a different path in the early days, sending the message that customers are important, but what we *really* care about is the stock price. Every decision, large and small, is cast within the culture of the company, and they made it clear again and again that customers and employees came first.

Not surprisingly, as the company got bigger, the rate of growth began to slow. First Bernie passed the mantle to Arthur, and when Arthur stepped down, the board recruited Robert Nardelli, one of Jack Welch's disciples who had just been passed over for the top spot at General Electric (GE). Nardelli came in with the charter of bringing operational discipline to a huge company that was focused on growth. To be fair, Home Depot needed operational discipline. As Nardelli described it, Home Depot was a big company that acted like it was an entrepreneurial company.[5] Nonetheless, the company was still very profitable, although growth slowed when the company passed $30 billion in sales.

Nardelli quickly put some of his GE lessons to work. But Home Depot was not GE, and his analytical style clashed with the free-spirited corporate culture at Home Depot. Perhaps more importantly, he didn't have a chance to learn and absorb the culture of the company before taking the helm. Unlike the general counsel who worked in the stores for two months to learn the ropes from the ground up, the new boss had landed in the top spot overnight. Culture clashes were inevitable.

Although Home Depot clearly needed operational discipline, some of the steps the new CEO initiated quickly undermined the culture Bernie and Arthur had painstakingly built. Like many new CEOs, he brought in his own people to replace seasoned veterans for key spots, while other senior managers left on their own. Of the 29 top people in the company, only one was still there a year later. With the institutional memory at the top of the company virtually wiped out, Home Depot's relentless focus on customers and associates gave way to focus on efficiency.

In a move to increase profits, Nardelli decided to jettison many long-time employees in the stores and replace them with part-time workers at lower pay. Nardelli increased the number of part-time employees to about half Home Depot's work force of 315,000; ostensibly to have more people available on weekends, but the move increased profits by cutting overall payroll costs.[6] This Chainsaw Al tactic was entirely focused on the bottom line—not adding value to the organization or improving the customer experience. The new CEO also implemented salary caps and passed on a greater share of benefit expenses to the employees. Those steps may seem like reasonable solutions during an economic downturn, but they were in direct opposition to the ethic that Bernie and Arthur had instilled in the company for years.

The results were disastrous. Morale plummeted, and as company veterans were replaced by inexperienced part-timers, the customer experience went downhill fast. Payroll wasn't the only thing that went down. Installing self-checkout lanes is another move that on the surface has good intentions—shorter checkout lines—but led to resentment from some customers already disappointed with poor customer service. In a company built on a culture of taking care of customers and associates, the structural changes aimed at increasing profits undermined the competitive advantages that Bernie and Arthur lived and breathed.

The result was entirely predictable. Home Depot did cut costs and boost profits in the short term. But in the process, the new boss inadvertently undercut what had been Home Depot's greatest asset—its strong customer service culture. The lower paid part-timers didn't have the knowledge or experience to deal with customer problems, and service levels suffered. After the short-term bump in profits, sales soon fell, and the new CEO who came in to improve profitability soon found himself under attack from the very Wall Street analysts with whom he was trying to win favor. Shareholders, analysts, and customers alike criticized the company in the media.

According to one senior executive who left the company, "Everything he's doing is counter-culture. It's bad for morale."[7] That could be dismissed as growing pains to be expected when any company's founders turn the reins over to the next generation of leadership. Home Depot's troubles, however, went much deeper. As one industry expert observed, "A lot of their problems have been self-inflicted. The issue wasn't consumer spending….The new CEO came, fired a number of people, brought back temps, and messed with the customer service culture. They lost market share as people went to other stores."[8]

This ill-fated change also coincided with a renewed attack from archrival Lowe's, which expanded into Home Depot's markets with a fresh new store design. By cutting costs in the wrong area, Home Depot stumbled badly. Two years after Nardelli's taking the reins at Home Depot, the company was still struggling. Sales at stores open more than a year were down 10 percent, and while the company brass pointed out that it was during a recession, Home Depot sales lagged rival Lowe's for seven straight quarters.[9]

At the company's annual shareholder meeting two years after taking charge, Nardelli told shareholders, "We are extremely troubled with the market reaction." He outlined new strategies, including new store formats, smaller inner-city stores, and expanded lamp and appliance sections to appeal to women. Even though he reversed the earlier move toward part-timers, his focus was still on the stock price, not on Home Depot's customers and employees. "We are absolutely committed to making sure we return this company to its prominent place in stock market performance," he said. That focus on the stock price is exactly what got the company in trouble to begin with. Shareholders weren't reassured, and Home Depot's stock, which was already down 20 percent for the year, fell another 7 percent.[10]

Watching from across town as the new owner of the Atlanta Falcons, Arthur Blank observed that Home Depot could boost sales and earnings by balancing an efficiency drive with a commitment to great customer service. "The success we had at Home Depot in its first 23 years was really based on focusing not on the bottom line but by focusing on customers, hearing what our associates were telling us about our business," Blank said. "If we put our associates and customers first, all good things in terms of bottom-line numbers to our shareholders really come from that."[11]

Look at the Bigger Picture

By all accounts, Home Depot and Costco have a lot in common. They both operate warehouse-size stores that sell merchandise at deep discounts, both had visionary founders who created a culture of focusing on customers, and both were built by their employees. While Home Depot stumbled, Costco CEO Jim Sinegal chose the opposite path—risking the ire of Wall Street by putting customers and employees ahead of profits.

While Home Depot was replacing experienced employees with part-timers to boost profits, a different story was unfolding in Issaquah, Washington. Costco, which has legions of loyal customers because it offers exceptional values, has an unusual philosophy. While most retailers price inventory as high as they can and still effectively sell it, Costco's membership plan legislates a minimal markup for most items. Instead of the 50 to 200 percent margins many retailers enjoy, Costco won't make more than 14 percent profit on any given item.

Acting on the belief that high wages produce high productivity, Costco pays hourly workers the top wages in retail. The average tenure of store managers is 15 years, and according to the National Retail Federation, Costco's turnover is a third of the retail industry's average, and shrinkage (that is, shoplifting and theft) is only 13 percent of the industry average.[12] The company promotes from within 99 percent of the time, which creates a career path and a level of cooperation among employees that sets Costco apart from its competitors.[13]

For years, it seemed that Costco could do no wrong. Sales and earnings were consistently growing, and the stock was consistently rising. In a 1999 interview, Jim warned that sooner or later there would be bumps in the road, saying that while the company "recognizes growth in earnings is important for the company and for long-term value to shareholders," he warned that Costco "will hit a hiccup, most assuredly; every business does."[14]

Costco hit that hiccup in 2002. In addition to higher health-care costs, worker's compensation expenses jumped 30 percent in California in one year. On top of that, the company responded to customer complaints about long checkout lines by adding more employees in many stores to help speed up lines at checkout counters.[15] These three factors increased expenses, and Costco issued an earnings warning and lowering guidance to Wall Street twice in six months. Not surprisingly, Costco's stock took a hit. Despite the earnings warning, Jim refused to bow to Wall Street pressure to increase profit margins by raising prices or cutting employee benefits.

Analysts were quick to point out that the company could make up the difference by raising prices—increasing the markup even slightly would yield an enormous profit increase. One analyst complained about the company's low prices, saying, "We believe it places club member interests too far ahead of shareholder interests." Jim refused to consider raising prices, still as true to his mission of providing value to Costco members as he was 25 years earlier when he cofounded the company. On the flip side, the analysts also blasted him for paying workers too much, suggesting that he cut employee pay or cut back on benefits. Jim's response is elegant in its simplicity. "If you hire good people, give them good jobs, and pay them good wages, generally something good is going to happen."[16]

Wall Street wizards may not agree with his methods, but they can't argue that Jim has built a powerhouse while staying true to his values. And he hasn't done badly for investors, either—$10,000 invested in Costco stock in 1992 was worth $43,564 a decade later. Between 1998 and 2003, sales grew 11.7 percent annually and earnings climbed 13.2 percent a year, even with the hiccup.[17] Despite the ebbs and flows of its stock price, Costco has consistently outperformed Sam's Club. Although Sam's Club had 71 percent more stores in the United States, Costco had 5 percent more sales in 2003 ($34.3 billion for Costco vs. $32.9 billion for Sam's Club). Furthermore, the average Costco store generates $112 million in sales, versus $63 million for the average Sam's Club.[18]

If the only goal of running a company is to make ever-increasing profits, Jim missed the boat. What he recognized—and the Wall Street analysts missed—is that changing direction simply to improve short-term profits would undercut everything he built. Even worse, it would undermine the culture and loyalty needed to keep the company strong and healthy in the years to come. "You have to take the shit with the sugar, I guess," Jim said. "We think when you take care of your customer and your employees, your shareholders are going to be rewarded in the long run. And I'm one of them; I care about the stock price. But we're not going to do something for the sake of one quarter that's going to destroy the fabric of our company and what we stand for."[19]

More Than a Pink Cadillac

Keeping your priorities straight isn't always easy, and in many cases, you may never know if you made the right decision. When faced with changes in your industry, or in the overall marketplace, make sure you make the right decision for the right reason. If you keep in mind the purpose of your company—the real reason you're there—it will help you to avoid the temptation of going for the easy money at the expense of your long-term competitive advantages.

In 1999, when Google was just getting off the ground and Borland was fighting for its life, a different kind of Internet story was unfolding in Dallas, inside a company many people would never think of as a technology leader. Mary Kay, Inc. is known to millions of people around the world as the company that gives its top salespeople pink Cadillacs.

Beyond that, many people don't know much about the company. They don't realize that with more than a million Independent Beauty Consultants worldwide, Mary Kay goes far beyond just selling cosmetics.

Mary Kay Ash's original vision of the company was to enrich women's lives. With that as the guiding principle, the company has grown to $1.6 billion in wholesale sales, and has averaged double-digit growth every year since Mary Kay founded the company in 1963. Very few billion-dollar businesses have been able to maintain that singular focus and crystal clear vision over such a long period of time. With the rise of the Internet and consumer e-commerce sites, the role of the company's independent sales force was called into question for the first time. The Internet not only had the potential to create a huge profit, but also had the possibility of creating turmoil and disruption for Mary Kay. The way the company handled its Internet launch serves as a valuable lesson in adopting new technology to improve operations without undermining the company's core strength.

Play to Your Strengths

One of Mary Kay's strengths over the years is its enormous network of independent beauty consultants worldwide. This army of beauty consultants sells beauty and skin-care products through personal relationships with customers in local communities. When the Internet exploded in the late 1990s, Mary Kay had more than 750,000 Independent Beauty Consultants around the globe. Like many other companies selling through an outside sales force, Mary Kay could have used the Internet as a force to increase profit margins. As Amazon.com and a host of other e-commerce companies rocketed onto the scene selling everything from airline tickets to dog food online, e-commerce looked like the wave of the future. Internet experts publicly speculated that Mary Kay would use the Internet to sell directly to consumers online, thus eliminating the need for an independent sales force.

As outside experts continually pointed out, Mary Kay could sell direct to consumers online using the company's Website, saving millions of dollars in commissions to its sales force. "Clearly every consultant that came into my office told me why I should use the Dell model," explains Kregg Jodie, Mary Kay's chief information officer.

They kept using Dell as an example, pointing out that Dell had cut out the middleman in the computer business. Kregg was quick to remind them that he had a Dell sales representative in his office once a month. From his vantage point, it wasn't the Internet that was the difference. From a business process, Dell had taken somebody out who wasn't adding value. "We clearly think our sales force is all of our value."[20]

Anyone close to the company knew that competing with their own sales force was never even a possibility. Instead of using the Internet to increase profits at the expense of its independent consultants, Mary Kay executives made a decision that was unfashionable at the time. They reaffirmed their commitment to the sales force and announced plans to launch MaryKay.com, with 100 percent of the effort dedicated to supporting the independent sales force.

There were two reasons why Mary Kay refused to even consider selling direct to consumers on MaryKay.com. As Kregg points out, "The reason for our company is enriching women's lives. That's related to giving them an opportunity, so it really didn't fit our business model and Mary Kay wouldn't have allowed it." The second reason was more practical. With the company completely focused on Independent Beauty Consultants, selling direct would have required it to change the operations at every level. It also would have required a major advertising effort necessary to drive traffic to the Website. That would be a major departure from the company's strategy, and directly counter to the grassroots relationships it had nurtured for decades. "We felt like that was still against our core fundamentals," Kregg said.

Mary Kay started online operations early, offering e-mail reports in 1995 and personal Web pages for beauty consultants in 1997. When the company launched MaryKay.com in 1999, it extended the personal home page program, allowing independent consultants to give out their own Web addresses and permitting them to accept orders from their customers online. Sales reps could also enter orders, view sales, and track shipments, and it provided a vehicle for communication to and from the field. Unlike other e-commerce sites, though, consumers could not order anything directly from the company. They could type in their zip code and find the independent consultants in their area, though, and place an order through one of them.

Behind the scenes, online orders from the new system were tied directly into the inventory picking system in the warehouse, cutting the time required to ship an order and decreasing errors to almost nothing. The new system eliminated much of the manual paperwork, both in the field and in the headquarters. Instead of calling in or faxing orders, most Independent Beauty Consultants enter orders directly, giving them more time to spend with their customers and less time filling out paperwork. The complexity is also greater than the typical e-commerce order. While Amazon.com typically has two or three line items in a $40 order, the average Mary Kay order has 40 to 60 line items for a $400 total.[21] The only thing MaryKay.com doesn't do is sell beauty products directly to customers.

As it turns out, Mary Kay's strategy was right on the money. The sales force has continued to grow, and now 90 percent of the company's orders—more than a billion dollars annually—come online. Equally important, the independent sales force had the unwavering support of the company throughout, and beauty consultants didn't have any of the anxiety or fear that they would be competing with the company. Instead, Mary Kay's model gives it the best of both worlds—a centrally planned system that uses technology to provide operational efficiencies, while still maintaining and supporting the individual relationships that have been the cornerstone of the company's success. Selling directly to the consumer online could never replace the personal relationships each beauty consultant has with her customers.

If the leaders at Mary Kay were primarily interested in maximizing profit margins, they might have made a different choice. Selling online directly to customers would have let them bypass their sales force and, at first glance, could have saved huge amounts of money. It also would have undermined Mary Kay's biggest competitive strength—a loyal army of dedicated people building personal relationships around the world. "We never seriously considered using the Internet to bypass our sales force," Kregg said. "It wouldn't fit our model. Our business is about our sales force, and our strongest competency as a company is our great network of people."[22]

Authentic Leadership

Former Medtronic CEO Bill George said it best, calling for "Authentic Leadership." In an opinion piece in the *Wall Street Journal*, Bill observed that we shouldn't be surprised by all the corporate scandals given Wall Street's focus: "an exaggerated and unbalanced emphasis on serving the short-term interests of shareholders, quarter after quarter. This mania for making Wall Street's numbers is at the heart of why some CEOs cheat and others have simply mismanaged. The public trust will not be restored until we have authentic leaders running our corporations and the wise heads on the Street realize how lasting shareholder value is created."[23]

By doing the right thing, you can truly build lasting value, as Costco and Mary Kay both demonstrated. The two primary factors for Costco's ongoing success are the two things that led Home Depot to stumble. Jim Sinegal showed courage and leadership, refusing to undercut Costco's core values—its employees and its customers—to increase profits. By having the courage to stand his ground and do the right thing for his people—both customers and employees—Costco shareholders will be far better off in the long run. In putting his own stamp on the company, Robert Nardelli inadvertently undercut Home Depot's culture of focusing on customers and associates, giving up one of its most important strategic advantages. That's not to say shareholders aren't important—of course they are. But focusing on rewarding shareholders (through the stock price) at the expense of customers and employees is a shortsighted strategy—and in the long run, isn't doing the shareholders any favors.

Mary Kay passed up an opportunity for a short-term profit, but reinforced its long-term strengths by remaining committed to the Independent Beauty Consultants who have made the company so successful. "Employees learn quickly whether they can trust their employer, and how that employer really feels about them," observed Stanford professor Jeffrey Pfeffer. "They figure it out not through the endless platitudes promulgated in literature from the human resources department, but by watching what the organization *does*."[24]

Chapter 13

Let Your Employees Call the Shots

In our society, we expect our leaders to know everything. When we have a question or something goes wrong, we want the boss to step forward and tell us what to do. The more dire the situation, the more people need a strong, confident leader at the helm. We want someone to turn to when things get tough. As a boss, it's easy to fall into this trap. We want to save the day. The problem is that in many situations, the leader doesn't have enough information to solve the problem. Very rarely are the issues black and white, and nobody can know everything that's going on in every part of the business. So what do you do?

The smart money would suggest tapping into the experience and knowledge of your subordinates by making them part of the solution. On one hand, you might just learn a few things. They could come up with ideas you haven't thought of. On the other hand, if they're part of the process, they're much more likely to take ownership of the outcome. In addition to boosting morale, getting employees involved in the decision-making process can give you access to a wealth of information. The challenge is to create an environment that encourages a free exchange of ideas and flow of candid feedback.

Why not let the people closest to the problem solve it? In a traditional organization, they send the problem uphill to someone higher—and further removed. That decision-maker has less information, and in a fast-moving environment, solutions will be imperfect at best. By creating a climate where employees on the front lines have the authority—and the autonomy—to correct the problem on the spot, the whole organization is faster, more responsive, and more efficient.

Let Them Solve Your Problems

Roger Berkowitz introduced a President's Advisory Council at Legal Seafoods to solicit input from hourly employees removed from the influence of the management. He took two hourly employees from every restaurant and put them in a room with just himself, a facilitator, and a recording secretary—no managers. Then he just started talking about issues in the restaurants, telling them he wanted honest feedback. "The great thing about hourly employees is that there is no politics involved. With no management there, they don't care what they say," Roger said. "I got some of the greatest feedback. Stuff I'd been struggling with for years, and they had the answers."

In addition to learning an enormous amount about what was going on in his own restaurants, he got insights and perspectives from a different side of the company. Based on that feedback, he made changes ranging from the menu items to the managers in restaurants. Nothing is off limits. In addition to being direct and honest, the feedback is also right on the money. After all, these are the people who are closest to the customers on a daily basis, and they know what's really going on.

"We sit here like eight wise men scratching our heads and say 'gee, I wonder why that didn't work?' You go down there and they tell you exactly why it didn't work," Roger said. "Sometimes we can get arrogant in our assumptions. That's an information band I have to constantly be in touch with."[1]

Rescuing Nissan

When Carlos Ghosn took over Nissan in 1999, it was heading for bankruptcy. Nissan had lost money and market share throughout the 1990s, and by the time Carlos arrived, it was carrying a staggering $19.4 billion in debt. Nissan spent more than $1 billion on interest payments alone, money it desperately needed to modernize its aging product line. The company was lacking strategic vision; it had no sense of urgency, a lackluster product line, overcapacity, and morale was at an all-time low.[2]

Nissan looked for buyers, but nobody was interested in inheriting those problems. In desperation, Nissan accepted a $5 billion cash injection from Renault in return for a 36.8 percent stake in the company. Renault got a chance to forge a powerful strategic alliance and the chance to return Nissan to profitability.[3] To do that, Renault tapped Carlos, a Brazilian-born, French-trained Lebanese with a solid track record of turning around companies in trouble. From the outset, Carlos had a huge handicap—he was a gaijin, or foreigner—with little hope for influence in Japan's insular culture.[4]

As an outsider, Carlos didn't speak Japanese, and he found himself running one of the world's largest automakers. He knew that in order to succeed, any plan to turn the company around would have to come from the people inside or it would fail, just like earlier turnaround efforts. He was also convinced that the people with years of experience there knew the company inside and out. They knew the problems and could offer the solutions Nissan needed. "I was non-Nissan, non-Japanese," Carlos said. "I knew that if I tried to dictate changes from above, the effort would backfire, undermining morale and productivity. But if I was too passive, the company would simply continue its downward spiral."[5]

Instead of imposing a turnaround plan from above, he got people from all parts of the company involved. Within a week of taking over, Carlos created nine cross-functional teams (CFT) to tackle vital functions of the company, including: purchasing, manufacturing, finance and cost, general and administrative, business development, sales and marketing, phase-out of products and parts, complexity management, and organization. To promote cooperation from the whole company, he assigned a cross section of employees to the teams, not just top executives. He also seeded the teams with key managers from Renault who came to Japan with him.[6]

The "pilot" of each team was a middle-level manager charged with chairing the meetings, driving the agenda, and keeping it on-track. Carlos challenged the CFT members to think freely and make specific recommendations on how to restore profitability and improve operations—immediately. "No sacred cows, no taboos, no constraints," Carlos instructed them.[7] By getting suggestions, ideas, and feedback from people throughout the company, Carlos got them to reevaluate areas that were previously considered off-limits.

Based on the recommendations of the teams, Carlos made sweeping changes at Nissan. Many of the measures were painful, including plant closures in Japan and dismantling the network of cross-shareholding with supplier companies. These steps were made with the clear goal of slashing purchasing costs, reducing debt, and reinvesting in improved vehicles.[8] Even though the workforce cuts were made through attrition, it still challenged the age-old concept of lifetime employment. Other recommendations ranged from cutting debt and selling off marginal assets to reducing the number of suppliers and giving priority to those who make a clear commitment to helping Nissan find ways to save money. He also upgraded the design team and the product strategy, investing heavily in a new line of vehicles that would excite customers.[9]

The results of the Nissan rescue plan were as swift as they were dramatic. Within 12 months, Nissan had reversed course and returned to profitability. Within two years, Nissan went from losing $5.7 billion to earning record net income of $2.98 billion.[10] "Something so drastic is too difficult for a Japanese manager," said Toyota Motors Corp. Chairman Hiroshi Okuda. "It's probably easier for Mr. Ghosn to do that because he has no bonds" with people in the group companies.[11]

While that may be true, it's also true that he could not have made sweeping changes without getting people from all parts of the company involved in making the decisions. Besides, as an outsider, there is no way he could have known everything going on in the company himself. The cross-functional teams were key to the Nissan Rescue Plan and the turnaround of the company.

Leaders of some other companies also pointed out that Carlos could not have made such drastic changes if Nissan wasn't in so much trouble. That may be true. But a company doesn't have to be facing a life-or-death crisis to get employees involved in the decision-making process. At Harley-Davidson, in fact, the exact opposite was true.

Harley Comes Roaring Back

When Harley-Davidson was struggling to survive in the early 1980s, the top-down command structure helped pull it back from the brink. The heavyweight motorcycle manufacturer was under serious pressure from Japanese competitors, who were producing higher quality motorcycles at lower costs, and Harley had a staggering debt load from a buyout. Forced into survival mode, Harley cut 40 percent of its workforce, and the remaining workers all took pay cuts and wage freezes. Management opened the books to the unions, who agreed that painful cuts were needed if the company hoped to survive. Everyone pulled together to save Harley, and their painful cuts, coupled with the successful launch of the Evolution engine and Softail product line—an elegant variation on the classic Harley design—brought the company back from the brink.[12]

When Rich Teerlink became CEO in 1988, he worried that he wouldn't be able to instill the same sense of urgency and teamwork to stay competitive over the long haul now that the threat of extinction was gone. When it was a matter of survival, everyone did whatever was necessary to save the company. Once the threat of extinction was gone, he was worried about complacency. How do you motivate employees and keep everyone working together now that the crisis is over? On top of that, Harley's union contract was coming up. Rich thought it would be best to work with the union and to try to get the union and management to understand and speak the same language.[13]

Instead of using the same top-down management style that was needed to save the company during the crisis, Rich was convinced he needed to get every employee to take responsibility for Harley to improve and prosper. To help move down that path, Rich brought in Lee Ozley, a management consultant with extensive experience in organizational change. That collaboration started Harley down the road to a partnership and a management style never before seen in a major manufacturing company.

Rich and Lee agreed that they needed to get employees to take ownership of the success of the company. "My belief is that the people are the only sustainable advantage we have," Rich explained. "What we leaders have to do is figure out ways to really show people that they are the sustainable competitive advantage. That's the environment we create."[14] Instead of simply announcing this new direction—a move that would be typical in a top-down management structure—they wanted people to help change the direction from the start.

They knew the starting point in a long process of changing the environment should be a vision of the ideal future of the company. Rich and Lee gathered 80 managers from all levels of the company to discuss the company's future in a process called Joint Vision. They held an intense three-day session, attended by 130 union and management leaders, to discuss the future of the company at the Milwaukee Airport Ramada Inn. They couldn't begin with a vision, though. First they had to identify what the values were, what issues they were trying to deal with, and who they serve. After developing the initial framework, they discussed and debated the "ideal view" of Harley in the future. In all, Harley committed more than 6,000 person-hours to the Joint Vision process.

Despite their efforts to move in a new direction, changing years of ingrained behaviors and attitudes wasn't easy. The unions were initially suspicious that the process was an attempt to subvert them. Employees tended to wait for instructions from above, instead of taking responsibility and making decisions in their areas.

The process took patience, commitment, and constant communication. After convening off-site with the Vision Group, teams of two— one person from management and one from the union—fanned out throughout the company to meet with employees in small groups. Rich and Tom Patterson, the president of Harley-Davidson, met with 50 separate groups of 40 employees at a time to communicate the new vision of the company, as well as to solicit input and ideas. They also met with more than 100 different union leaders to discuss the business process, and they took the message to the dealer network, key suppliers, and investors.[15] Continuing to reinforce the message, Harley created four-hour training modules on each of the key topics—values, issues, stakeholders, and vision.

"We had patience to not just say it, but to create the supporting structures," Rich said. "The business process is a major supporting structure. It gives everybody an opportunity to understand what's going on in the business down here, what your position is, and an opportunity to influence it if you want to."[16] The process was much like turning around an aircraft carrier, not a speed boat; it took a long time to make a gradual turn, but in the end, the results were dramatic.

Reinventing the Wheel

In 1993, Harley undertook one of the most revolutionary management changes of all—eliminating the structure and hierarchy found in almost every major corporation. In most companies, the people in charge of each department have almost no direct contact with their counterparts in other areas of the company.

Instead of traditional hierarchies such as production, sales, marketing, accounting, and customer support, they reorganized the company into three "natural work groups": *create demand*, *produce products*, and *provide support*. Harley also eliminated all senior vice-president positions, which tend to be fiefdoms jealously guarding power. Instead, each circle is comprised of eight or nine managers, with a "coach" to guide (but not direct) them. The *produce products* circle is responsible for engineering and production; the *create demand* circle handles sales and marketing; and the *provide support* circle is in charge of human resources, and financial and legal functions.

Tying it all together is a Functional Leadership Group, which is comprised of six managers elected by their peers from within the circles. The Functional Leadership Group, plus the president of the company, would act as the Leadership and Strategy Council to address things affecting all the circles, including budgets, strategic plans, and policies affecting all employees.[17]

The idea of this radical structural change was to get the different parts of the company to work together, sharing information and ideas to benefit everyone. People who had historically taken their ideas, problems, and complaints up the chain of command were encouraged to work directly with the right people to get things done. Decisions began to be made as close to the source of the problem or topic as possible. Leaders who had previously occupied formal command-and-control positions were being transformed from "commanders" into "facilitators and coaches."[18]

Under the old system, if a worker on the shop floor discovered a problem with a part from the supplier, he would tell his manager, who would report it to the supervisor, who would tell the director. The director would talk to a director in purchasing, who would send it back downhill to the purchasing manager to discuss with a supplier. Under the new system where everyone takes responsibility, the worker who discovered the problem would pick up the phone and call the supplier directly.

The results have been dramatic. In an era where critics contend that manufacturing companies in the United States can't be competitive anymore, Harley delivered 18 consecutive years of record revenues and earnings.

A New View of Working Together

In the mid-1990s, Harley-Davidson was faced with a new problem. The company that was back from the brink a decade before didn't have enough production capacity to meet demand for its motorcycles. Instead of opening a new plant with non-union employees, Harley appointed a committee of three people to select the new location—one manufacturing executive from the company and two union representatives. The committee selected Kansas City as the new location, and immediately got employees involved in the planning process. Groups of hourly employees, working without supervisors, teamed up with engineers to design the entire assembly process. Some of the breakthrough concepts they developed were later introduced in Harley's other factories in Wisconsin and Pennsylvania.[19]

While some people may question this approach, arguing that those decisions are too important for lower-level employees, that's exactly why Harley let them call the shots. Who better to help plan the assembly line than the people who would actually be working on it?

Harley took the relationship a step further. The leaders of the International Association of Machinists (IAMs) and Paper, Allied-Industrial, Chemical & Energy Workers International (PACE) share an office with the plant manager. When Harley CEO Jeff Bleustein addressed shareholders at the annual meeting, Tom Buffenbarger, the international president of the IAM, and Boyd Young, the international president of PACE, shared the podium with him to discuss the power of partnering at Harley-Davidson.[20]

"This is a true partnership where we make joint decisions on this company," Joe Cooper, grand lodge representative for the IAM explains. "Harley workers are making decisions out on the shop floor. They're helping make the company profitable and at the same time it's giving job security for them." As Joe points out, the old way of doing business is obsolete. "If unions and companies in the manufacturing sector—or in any sector—are going to survive in this global economy, they have to get their heads out of the sand and work in a new direction. We can no longer do business as usual."[21]

As Rich points out, no leader is smart enough to lay out all the rules, all the objectives, and all the possible scenarios. If you try, employees will follow your instructions blindly. "People really want to do a great job, and when they don't, it's probably because of the environment they live in," he explains. "The top-down command and control environment does not inspire me to do great things. It inspires me to be compliant. That says that I, as a leader, have to give up the power."[22]

A Little Appreciation Goes a Long Way

Getting employees to take responsibility for the success of the company doesn't require a complete overhaul of the organization. When Green Mountain Coffee Roasters was going through a major growth phase, Bob Stiller realized costs were rising almost as rapidly as sales. Knowing he needed to tighten up the operation, he decided to try a new approach. Instead of dictating solutions from the top down, he used a new approach called Appreciative Inquiry (AI). AI was developed by David Cooperrider, a professor at the Weatherhead School of Management at Case Western Reserve University in Cleveland, as a positive approach to change that focuses on the company's best attributes and builds on them.[23]

At Green Mountain Coffee Roasters, Bob Stiller found that while the top-down management approach works, it doesn't inspire creativity and motivation. AI is unique because it gets people charged up by building positive energy. Using AI, Green Mountain kicked off the "25¢ Challenge" with the goal of reducing operating costs by 25 cents for each pound of coffee, effectively lowering costs 7 percent. The employees responded enthusiastically, coming up with a variety of different cost-saving ideas that helped them hit their goal. "In sports, some people won't even look at mistakes," Bob explains. "If you're out playing golf and you say, 'I don't want to hit the ball in the woods,' that's where it goes. You always want to be building energy off the positive and where you want to go."[24]

After the success of the 25¢ Challenge, Green Mountain did AI once or twice a year, each with a different theme, such as "Living our Purpose and Principles for delivering growth and value." In every case, the goal is to encourage employee involvement to improve the company. As a result of one employee's idea, Green Mountain produced a cobranded line of fair trade and organic coffee with Newman's Own. That partnership opened more doors for them—getting Green Mountain coffee into several major supermarket chains such as Publix and Shop 'n Save, after several years of trying to get in unsuccessfully on their own.

Other companies have been just as successful using Appreciative Inquiry to build positive change. At Roadway Express, a team of short-haul drivers came up with 12 cost-cutting and revenue-generating ideas. For example, workers at the Akron distribution center realized that some trucks carried more fuel than needed, adding unnecessary weight. That suggestion saved the company $118,000 a year.[25] Hunter Douglas's window fashions division used AI as the foundation of its "Focus on Excellence" initiative. The ideas employees generated saved the division $3.5 million in the first year.[26] "People are dying at every level of a company to be tapped on the shoulder and asked for their opinion," David Cooperrider said.[27]

Get Employees Involved in Making Decisions

When Carlos Ghosn created teams at Nissan to try to address the crisis facing the company, many people were reluctant to do anything. They had never been asked for their opinions before, and they didn't know what to do. Rich Teerlink had the same exact problem at Harley-Davidson. Harley workers were used to the "us vs. them" approach, and decisions had always come from the top down. Trying to change those attitudes took time and continual reinforcing.

Both Carlos and Rich created new decision-making frameworks to put authority in the hands of the people doing the work, and both consistently reinforced the message. It took a lot of work to overcome old habits, but, in the end, the results were astounding. Nissan rebounded from the brink of bankruptcy to become one of the most profitable automakers in the world. Harley-Davidson dispelled the notion that manufacturers can't be competitive in the United States, racking up 18 consecutive years of record profits. Roger Berkowitz used his President's Advisory Council at Legal Seafoods to get ideas and feedback directly from hourly employees on the restaurant floor. Bob Stiller used the Appreciative Inquiry at Green Mountain Coffee Roasters to tap into the creativity and energy of his employees while focusing on positive change. Like Roger, Bob recognized that the people closest to customers on a daily basis have a lot of ideas about how to improve the experience.

Getting employees to take charge isn't an overnight process. You can't wave a magic wand and have people completely engaged. Some managers will resist, unwilling to give up what they perceive as their authority. And some employees will be reluctant to step forward, because they are unconvinced about the company's true intentions—or just unsure what to do or how to do it. By creating a structure that encourages employees to take responsibility for the success of the company—and making an active effort to get them involved—you'll get benefits you never dreamed of.

Regardless of the method, the message is clear—the old top-down command structure just doesn't do it anymore. Leaders who insulate themselves from feedback at the grassroots level are going to make imperfect decisions at best. Giving workers a key role in the process will go a long way toward getting everyone moving in the same direction together.

Chapter 14

Help Them Sell and You'll Both Win

Inside most companies, sales are the benchmark by which everything is measured. When sales go up, everyone inside the company is rewarded and life is good. Not surprisingly, increasing sales naturally becomes the focus. Instead of focusing on making the numbers by selling more this quarter, smart companies make much more in the long run by figuring out how to help *their customers* make more money.

It's a common practice for vendors to load up a dealer or retailer with their product, even to the point where retailers are buying more than they can possibly sell. They make their numbers, the boss is happy, and life is good. Except for one minor detail. If the supply chain is now awash in their product, they're creating more problems down the road. Even if the inventory isn't perishable—meaning not just that it will spoil, but it may become outdated or out of season—at best, this creates peaks and valleys in ordering, which makes life difficult for those actually producing it.

Even though you may make less money in the short run, creating a climate of trust with your customers is far more valuable in the long run. Instead of trying to get your customers to buy more, you can create a sustainable advantage by finding ways to make your distribution partners successful.

Ask What They Need—
Not What You Need to Sell Them

When Lou Pritchett arrived in Manila to take over as president of the Philippines Manufacturing Company (PMC), the Procter & Gamble (P&G) subsidiary was on the verge of bankruptcy. Although Filipino consumers strongly preferred two P&G soaps, Safeguard and Camay, they were both dead last in sales against competing brands. Sales were stalled, the company was mired in debt, and accounts receivable were going through the roof.

Lou quickly discovered that 100 percent of the company's efforts in the previous decade had been to push more product out the door. The managers and everyone downstream were rewarded based on the amount of soap they sold to wholesalers and retailers, but the company made no effort to help its distribution partners sell the products to consumers. As sales quotas increased, PMC salespeople pushed harder to get distributors and retailers to buy more—even when inventory was already stacking up in the warehouses.

Even worse, the warehouses where the distributors stored their inventory weren't air conditioned, and the temperature inside often got as high as 140 degrees. Because they were made with coconut oil, the bars of soap that were fine coming off the production line began to deteriorate and smell bad after sitting in a hot warehouse for several months.[1] Sales faltered as the backlog increased, and PMC managers pushed even harder to sell more soap, offering sales incentives and discounts that caused the backlog to pile up even higher.

Although he knew it would be a painful solution, Lou immediately announced a moratorium on selling. He then ordered his sales organization not to accept any orders from customers who had more than a four-week supply of Safeguard or Camay. If a customer had a five-week supply, the salesperson got a bonus for *not* selling them more soap. Not surprisingly, PMC missed its sales goal by 40 percent that year.

Once they cleared the backlog and made sure all the inventory in the system was fresh, they started selling again. Sales quickly picked up, and within 18 months, Safeguard and Camay were the number one and two selling brands in the Philippines. As sales volume and profits grew to record highs, there were other direct benefits. Inventories and receivables were substantially lower, sales forecasts were more accurate, and bank borrowing decreased substantially. And, of course, morale in the company soared.[2]

Be Careful What You Reward

Instead of simply selling distributors and retailers as much product as they could, Lou turned PMC around by focusing on turnover selling—shipping their customers only as much as they needed, when they needed it, and helping them be more effective at selling it. "I helped create an environment that allowed the organization to do what it was capable of doing. It was that basic."[3] PMC focused on the customer and moved away from the "sell, sell, sell at any cost" mentality. Now it viewed customers as partners and sold them only what they needed.

As Lou points out, the first place to start looking for trouble is the internal reward recognition system. "What are people really rewarded and recognized for doing or not doing? You'll be amazed when you go back and examine those companies and you realize that so many companies are rewarding and recognizing their people for things that actually damage the operation that support it," Lou said. "If your customer is consuming 100, but you're shipping him 125, which is what we were doing in the Philippines, you haven't accomplished a damn thing. With our reward recognition system, you were going to get a big bonus if you shipped him 125. And you didn't worry about what it did to his costs or his inventory, or the condition of his stock as it did in the Philippines if you overloaded him and put this stuff in there."[4]

Changing the Game at eMachines

In taking over eMachines, Wayne Inouye stopped shipping new computers loaded with potentially incompatible software programs, and he turned the customer support model upside down. Another major change he made that was key to saving the company was changing the way eMachines worked with retailers. After earning his stripes as the head merchant at Good Guys and Best Buy, he knew a lot about selling computers and electronics.

At Best Buy, Wayne was frustrated by PC makers who guessed what options buyers wanted without getting feedback from customers or retailers.[5] Prior to his arrival, eMachines did exactly the same thing—guessing what customers wanted, then shipping it and hoping that it sold. Because they had price protection and stock balancing provisions, retailers would take what eMachines sent them, later sending back anything they couldn't sell. Sales were hit-and-miss, and eMachines lost a ton of money when retailers returned the unsold computers.

The other side of the equation, Wayne knew all too well, was that retailers couldn't tailor computer configurations according to customer demand. With an array of options ranging from extra memory and graphics accelerators to DVD burners and sound cards, retailers didn't know how to forecast demand for a variety of different features. On top of that, they had very little or no control over the supply chain, so even when they did know when customers wanted specific features, they had trouble getting them.[6] Instead, the PC makers would decide what to build and expect customers to buy it.

Instead of perpetuating what he considered to be bad behavior, Wayne turned this model upside down. First, he stopped offering price protection and stock balancing—a move that made him unpopular with retailers at first. Instead, he presented another alternative that he thought made more sense. Using a model initially developed at Best Buy, he had the product managers at eMachines analyze the sales data to see which computer configurations customers were actually buying. This "sell-through" data was a much more accurate indication of customer demand, and Wayne shared this detailed data with his retail partners to make sure they were ordering the optimal configurations.

Finding the Value

The key to making sense of all the different options available was a system Wayne called the "Value Equation." At Best Buy, he could see all the trends in peripherals and order configurations accordingly. At eMachines, he turned that idea around 180 degrees to view it from a manufacturer's perspective. The Value Equation let eMachines calculate the dollar value of computer configurations, and then look at the different configurations based on actual sell-through data in a variety of channels. For example, there are times in the retail channel when customers can add more memory for $30, but the extra memory may cost the manufacturer $32.[7] Customers don't place a lot of value in the extra memory, and, in fact, many want different features such as a DVD burner or a bigger hard drive instead. Trying to predict these preferences was difficult, and spending money on features customers didn't care about cost money but didn't add value.

By collecting detailed sell-through data from each retailer, eMachines showed retailers what features were most popular and how much customers were willing to pay for them. In the process, Wayne turned forecasting from guesswork into a science. Every week, eMachines analyzed enormous amounts of data to decide when to introduce new computers and what features to include in each configuration. [8]

As the retailers realized that the new system was actually more efficient and increased sales, they got on board. Retailers won because sales and profits increased, and they didn't get stuck with unsold inventory. At the same time, eMachines increased sales and eliminated the need for costly returns. By working closely with his retail partners and sharing his detailed analysis, Wayne made sure eMachines was making PCs with the features customers wanted, which improved efficiency and profits for both partners.

Wayne's strategy of forecasting demand based on actual sales, and sharing that information with retail partners to make better decisions, was a key factor in the company's turnaround. The company that was losing $200 million a year and was delisted by the NASDAQ when Wayne took over logged eight profitable quarters in a row. Inventory turn increased from four times a year to more than 70, and eMachines passed Gateway as the number-three PC maker in the United States.[9] Recognizing a good thing, Gateway acquired eMachines and named Wayne CEO of the combined company.

Looking at Your Customers in a Different Way

After 10 years in business, Brighton Collectibles, which was originally called Leegin Leather, was a moderately successful manufacturer of leather goods sold in small retail shops around the country. Year after year, sales were stuck between $9 and $10 million. It didn't matter what the company did, it never managed to break the $10 million mark. Because Jerry Kohl refused to sell to department stores in favor of small, independent retailers, some people openly wondered if the company even had a future.

After attending a program at Harvard Business School for company owners and presidents, Jerry made two changes in the way the company operated. The next year, Leegin broke the magic number for the first time, recording $10.8 million in sales. Sales leaped to $15 million the year after that, and then $20 million the following year.[10] The upward trajectory continued year after year, growing to $35 million, $50 million, and $65 million. By 2003, sales grew to $160 million. The company is still run by the same management team and still sells to the same small retail shops. Brighton didn't land a deal with Wal-Mart or Target, and it still doesn't sell to major accounts. It didn't even advertise. As Jerry explains, the breakthrough came in the way Brighton works with its customers.

Help Them Make More Money

Instead of trying to get shop owners to *buy* more leather belts, Jerry changed his focus to *help them sell* more leather belts. This subtle distinction changed the nature of their relationship. Jerry knew that in order to grow, he had to differentiate Brighton from all the other companies making belts. Having started a small T-shirt shop with his wife when they were still in high school, he was committed to helping the "little guys," which also meant not selling to department stores. The downside was that meant a lot of small orders from independent mom-and-pop shops.

In order to be successful, Jerry realized he would have to learn where his customers were making money, then help them make even more. By changing the way it operates, Jerry made Brighton an indispensable partner for hundreds of independent retail shops throughout the country. More than anything else, he had to create a level of service and a relationship his customers couldn't find anywhere else.

The first thing Jerry wanted to do was help his customers improve their own operations. Because there was no software available at the time to do what he wanted, Jerry bought a computer and taught himself to program. He wrote a software program to track sales for his customers, and later teamed up with another programmer to refine and improve it. His idea was to increase his sales by helping his customers operate more efficiently.

Until that time, store owners placed orders in a manner much like throwing darts—they guessed. Most companies sell through distributors or wholesalers, relying on customers to make their own buying decisions. If a vendor introduced three new styles of belts, for example, the owner might look through a catalog and order 10 of each. When it came time to reorder, they would replace whatever they sold so they still had 10 of each, or they might order 10 more of each.

Sell With Them—Not to Them

Jerry changed all that. When a Brighton sales rep arrives in a store, the first thing he or she does is count the products in stock and take inventory. Armed with a laptop and a detailed history of the store's sales by category, style, and color, the sales rep can then go over the actual numbers with the store owner and make recommendations for the next order. For example, if brown belts are selling much better then black belts, the sales reps can make recommendations accordingly. If the store isn't selling many men's belts, there is no reason to order more. They can also show the customer the most successful products at other stores in their region. By providing detailed information and showing the shop owners what's selling and what's not, Brighton helps them make smarter buying decisions and actually *make more money*.

Brighton has 100 full-time salespeople who call on small shop owners every day. By using software to track each retailer's sales, the Brighton sales reps walk in the door armed with more knowledge about the store than the store owners themselves. By sharing the detailed information about what is moving and where, what they sold in the same period last year, Brighton helps the small store owners make more money. For many shops, the belts and leather goods have gone from an overlooked corner to one of the most profitable areas of the store.

As Jerry points out, most store owners are nice people who wanted to start their own business, but most don't have any formal business training. They don't know about cash management, forecasting, and inventory turns. As the largest vendor for many of these stores, Brighton wants to make sure they are successful. "Our number-one goal is to make sure you don't buy too much," Jerry explains. "If you buy too much, you're not going to have any money and the store is going to be filled up and you're going to be mad at me."[11]

By keeping the orders smaller, the shop owners can turn over their inventory faster and improve cash flow. How many other companies will tell their customers to order less? At the same time, the orders Brighton dealers do place are based on a solid understanding of what's selling and how quickly it's moving, which gives Brighton dealers a level of inventory management and sophistication they couldn't afford on their own.

The other thing Jerry changed was the back office. Instead of having one department in charge of customer service, another for accounting, etc., he broke down the walls and assigned people to handle everything necessary to take care of a specific retail shop. Every time someone from that store calls, they deal with the same two people, whether it's to place an order, make a payment, or deal with a problem. Instead of trying to sell more, Jerry built Brighton into a phenomenal success story by helping his customers succeed.

Beer Goes High Tech

Helping your channel partners be more effective works in almost any industry. Anheuser-Busch built an extranet called BudNET to help its beer distributors operate more efficiently and increase sales. By effectively using technology in a low-tech industry, BudNET offers Anheuser-Busch and its distribution partners the same kind of data Wayne Inouye used to forecast demand for PCs at eMachines and Jerry Kohl gave Brighton dealers. Several thousand drivers and sales reps check inventory at retailers throughout the country, entering it in their handheld computers and transmitting over wireless phones on the spot.

Not long ago, sales reps and distributors would return from their routes with stacks of invoices, which they would enter into the computer at the brewery to upload. The brewery, in turn, would compile monthly reports to see what was selling. Chairman August Busch III changed all that, vowing to make his company the leader in using technology to track his customers' buying habits. BudNET gives detailed, up to the minute reports on sales, inventory, and displays at thousands of stores nationwide.[12]

Retail outlets don't even need to place orders anymore; BudNET allows drivers to replace inventory that's been sold, and tailor the stock in each store to the local tastes in the area. "Honestly? I think I know more about these guys' businesses than they do," one driver said. "At least in the beer section."[13] By tracking what beer drinkers are buying, and when and where they're buying it, BudNET has helped Anheuser-Busch prosper during a very tough period. When beer industry volume was down 1.6 percent, Anheuser-Busch volume rose 1.2 percent, topping 50 percent of total market share for the first time.[14]

Make Their Lives Easier

Nextel applied a similar principle to the wireless industry to streamline its distribution system and make life easier for its retail partners. While most cellular phones allow a simple over-the-air programming process, programming Nextel phones is more complicated because Nextel offers group calling using its direct connect feature. Even after giving dealers special training on programming, the activation process was still slower and more complicated. Furthermore, Nextel dealers and distributors had the same problem as every other retailer—correctly predicting what models customers would want and making sure the right phones were in stock.

Nextel addressed all these issues at once by changing the distribution process to help its channel partners. Instead of buying phones in advance and activating them when customers come in, Nextel introduced a program called Value Added Distribution (VAD). When a customer orders a phone, all the dealer has to do is enter the customer's activation information online and the order is processed electronically. The phone arrives the next morning by 10:30 a.m. activated, charged, and ready to use—completely eliminating the old way of doing things. Nextel handles all the activation, programming, inventory, and shipping.

Nextel's VAD makes it easier for retail salespeople because they no longer have to worry about programming, activating, and troubleshooting phones. Nextel's dealers and distributors, in turn, no longer have to stock every phone in every location, which eliminates one of their biggest operating expenses.

"It's fantastic," said Ray Rodriguez, president and CEO of Northstar Wireless, a Nextel Master Distributor. "It lowers our inventory carrying costs and makes it easier for our dealers."[15]

You'll Make More Money If You Help Them

As Lou Pritchett discovered, PMC could overload their distributors with inventory, but it hurt both of them in the long run. By bringing the entire operation to a screeching halt, Lou cleared out the inventories and started all over again, selling distributors and retailers only the amount of inventory they really needed. By treating his partners like partners, and not blindly pushing inventory on them, Lou turned the ship around and substantially grew sales over the long haul.

Jerry Kohl grew Brighton from $9 million to $180 million in sales by finding ways to help his dealers be more successful. Wayne Inouye applied the exact same principle at eMachines, working closely with his channel partners to optimize the inventory based on actual demand, instead of guessing what configurations to make and then hoping they'll sell. Anheuser-Busch and Nextel applied the same principles, streamlining their operations, reducing inventory carrying costs, and greatly improving efficiency in their distribution channels. In each case, the companies that made a concerted effort to make life better for their distribution partners also got the same benefits themselves.

If your only goal is to increase sales right now, you're missing a bigger opportunity in the long run. Rewarding salespeople based on how much product they can push out into the channel, regardless of what happens to it after that, is asking for trouble. Instead, focus on ways to help your distribution partners be successful, and you'll create a sustainable advantage and sell a lot more in the long run.

Chapter 15

Make Outside Partners
Part of Your Team

Although customers and employees are both vital to any company's success, there is another group of stakeholders that's equally important to the company's success—the outside partners. Partners can include strategic partners, vendors or suppliers, franchisees, or anyone else on whom your business depends. If you have a good relationship, outside partners can help smooth out the bumps during rocky times—whether it's tight cash flow when you need to stretch out payments, or a rush order that you absolutely have to have yesterday.

Most people view their vendors and suppliers as a necessary evil, a sparring partner to square off against periodically—and the vendor relationship usually reflects that. Aside from getting a fruit basket during the holidays, these relationships yield little friendship or personal contact. Perhaps the problem stems from the actual word "supplier." It sounds expendable, interchangeable, and impersonal. In most cases, the partner with more throw weight tends to call the shots.

Most people view partnerships from the perspective of "what's in it for me?" The partnership makes sense only as long as it offers me something I can't easily get on my own. The problem is that this viewpoint creates an adversarial approach that eventually causes both parties to suffer. In a few cases, where both parties make a concerted effort to truly create an alliance, the whole can be greater than the sum of the parts. If you bend over backward to get your outside partners involved, you'll both be better off.

A Long-Term Relationship Is More Valuable Than a Short-Term Profit

Few companies treat their vendors better than Dave Gold and 99 Cents Only stores. In more than 30 years, 99 Cents Only has never canceled a single purchase order. If 99 Cents Only buyers say they'll buy something and find out later they could get it cheaper somewhere else, they still take it. They don't renegotiate and they don't change their mind after the fact. Dave still maintains the long forgotten retail practice of open vendor days. Anybody with something to sell them can show up on Tuesday or Thursday morning with no appointment and meet with the buyers. In addition to giving Dave and his team a chance to actually see and touch the products people want to sell them, it also goes a long way toward building relationships. While many companies treat vendors like a necessary evil, Dave and his team bend over backward to treat them right, because they know how valuable those relationships are.

Victor and Janie Tsao built Linksys on the strength of his relationships with his manufacturing partners in Taiwan. He started small, building trust and maintaining a balanced and profitable relationship for them both. If a Linksys product was a winner, they both made money. If it flopped, they both lost money. By treating his partners like partners, instead of a random supplier to be squeezed whenever possible, he built a working relationship that was crucial to the company's success as Linksys grew from a $6 million mom-and-pop business to a $500 million industry leader.

Harley-Davidson goes to great lengths to make suppliers part of the team, including setting up a Supplier Advisory Council for top-level suppliers and Harley staffers. The Council focuses on three goals: doubling quality, cutting product development time, and lowering the cost of goods. Instead of squeezing suppliers' margins, though, Harley works with them to cut costs through innovation and efficiency. One supplier came up with the idea to reroute the water in the new liquid-cooled engine design, saving $50 a bike. Another supplier learned that Harley spent $1 million a year processing returns of damaged engine-head covers, and developed a thin piece of adhesive-backed foam to slip under the chrome during assembly, which prevented the damage at a cost of a few cents per unit. That solution saved Harley more than $900,000 each year.[1]

The key to successful relationships is to find the balance where both sides win, even if you aren't making every possible nickel of profit. In-N-Out Burger has used the same supplier for its hamburger buns for more than 50 years. You can't buy that kind of relationship. Both companies are better off by working closely together, and both profit when the other does well. It's far better to create and cultivate a relationship that will continue to be profitable over the long term.

Changing the Tide at P&G

In 1987, Lou Pritchett, the vice president of sales at Procter & Gamble, went on a canoe trip with Sam Walton to propose an unprecedented partnership with Wal-Mart. Until that time, senior executives at P&G *never* talked to Wal-Mart. Although sales reps from eight different P&G divisions called on Wal-Mart, the senior management seemed to go to great lengths to ignore their largest customer. When Wal-Mart named P&G as its vendor of the year, it was so unimportant to P&G that they ignored the honor and didn't even bother picking up the award. As Sam Walton pointed out, P&G sold more products to Wal-Mart than they did to the entire nation of Japan.

From Lou's vantage point after 30 years in the company, P&G's entire view of the world was its unquestioned belief in in the superiority of its product and its advertising copy. Little else mattered. Three generations of Procter & Gamble managers had grown up in this environment, and the idea that top management should have anything to do with customers was completely foreign. After all, they had a huge sales organization to "handle" customers—why should they bother?[2]

After learning his lesson turning around the Philippines Manufacturing Company, Lou was convinced P&G would benefit if it had closer working relationships with its customers. He made a personal commitment to change the company's historical relationship—or lack thereof—with its customers. Deciding to take it to the top, he arranged a canoe trip with Sam Walton to discuss a new idea in partnering between the two companies.

Sam was so shocked by Lou's approach that he decided to go along. Besides, he was curious to see what a P&G executive was like in person, never having met one before. As they paddled down the river together,

Sam mentioned how disappointed he was in the way P&G had treated Wal-Mart. "Your people act like a bunch of guys who just don't have time for us."[3]

One thing that drove Sam crazy was salespeople who showed up to try to push whatever product they decided would be on sale that month, with no regard to the retailer's strategy or merchandising plans. "Let me give you an example," Sam said. "I know you've got a formula for making Tide. Suppose a chemical salesman called on you every 30 days and said, 'Hey, I've got $200 a ton off on sulphur this month. Why don't you change your Tide formula? Why don't you put more sulphur in it this month?'" That's exactly what P&G—and other manufacturers—were doing when they showed up trying to sell the flavor of the month without first bringing the retailers into the equation.

Sam and Lou both agreed that their relationship was completely adversarial. Each company focused on its customer, but by not consulting with each other, each was missing a huge opportunity. If they could work together to share sales and inventory information, they could increase efficiency and drive costs out of the system on both sides.

As Lou pointed out, they could work together so that when a box of Tide or Crest toothpaste or Pampers crossed the scanner in a Wal-Mart store, that information was sent straight back to Procter & Gamble so it could start making more. Wal-Mart could turn its inventory faster and decrease its costs, while P&G wouldn't have to load warehouses with products that just sat there in case an order came in. By making decisions based on actual sales instead of guesswork, both companies would benefit. Working together as partners, they could drive the inventory out of the system, and cut costs on each side. Back in those days, no two multi-billion-dollar companies had ever done anything like that before.

The opportunity Lou and Sam agreed on during their canoe trip became a revolutionary partnering agreement between P&G and Wal-Mart. Within three months, the top 10 officers from P&G flew to Bentonville, Arkansas, for a two-day strategy session with Wal-Mart. Within six months, the two companies created a joint working group with teams from each company, including sales, marketing, accounting, manufacturing, distribution, and systems, to work directly with their counterparts to develop a new system of working together.[4] The seeds from that initiative have grown into one of the most sophisticated inventory systems in the world. Wal-Mart extended this partnering agreement to other suppliers as well, and Wal-Mart's Retail Link now allows it to share inventory and sales data real-time with all of its vendors throughout the world.[5]

By working together as partners, each company cut operating costs and increased profits. In Sam's words, they rationalized the distribution system. In a letter to Lou the year before he died, Sam wrote, "I think back on our first canoe trip and how we evolved our partnership process with Procter & Gamble. It was one of the best things that ever happened to our company, and I think time bears out that many other companies are beginning to view the supplier as an important partner."[6]

Turning Adversaries Into Allies

Intuit had a different problem to overcome with its distribution partners. Despite all its success with Quicken, Intuit created a built-in channel conflict because it sold the same software over the phone that retail stores sold to customers. Retailers are naturally wary of a vendor who competes with them. Because it sold direct to customers, Intuit's multi-channel strategy risked alienating retailers. In essence, Intuit was competing with its customers. Scott Cook could have simply said, "Too bad, that's the way we're going to do it," as many other companies have done; instead, Intuit took a novel approach to promote Quicken to retailers and cultivate relationships with them.

To overcome this suspicion and make retailers part of the team, Intuit implemented a program called the National Sales Tour in the early 1990s. When Intuit launched a new version or product, most employees who weren't tied to the phones traveled to retail stores all over the country to train store salespeople on the new product. People from different parts of the country fanned out to visit retailers in their home states, which gave them a chance to visit family and friends at the same time. Although this program cost a lot of time and money for a small company, Scott was convinced it was a good investment.

Intuit bent over backward to make its retail outlets feel like partners, and its efforts paid off. Retailers who were already happy with Quicken's low return rate liked the company even more after a National Sales Tour visit. The National Sales Tour also gave employees another one-on-one interaction with customers, again reinforcing the company's relentless focus on the customer. As one programmer said, "My code is there on the shelf, at the front lines. Seeing it there and the enthusiastic response of the retail sales teams convinces me that my work really matters."[7]

When Microsoft launched Money, its personal finance program, Intuit suddenly found itself in a battle for its very existence. Microsoft had a long history of rolling right over smaller competitors who got in its way, and Intuit was in the unenviable position of being first in line as the next victim. As it turned out, Intuit's strong relationships with retailers became a pivotal weapon in fighting off the juggernaut from Redmond when Microsoft launched Money for Windows.

Breaking its long-standing policy of not preannouncing software, Intuit announced that it would soon release its new version of Quicken for Windows. Intuit also did something unprecedented; it sent out coupons to all existing Quicken customers, but instead of asking them to buy directly through Intuit, they gave a mail-in rebate for Quicken for Windows bought through retail stores. Retailers who were already happy with Quicken were now thrilled that Intuit was driving traffic into their stores. Many retailers recommended that customers hold off on Microsoft Money, which created lists of people waiting for the new version of Quicken to come out.[8]

Despite all the defensive moves by Intuit, the deciding factor was the product itself. Money was loaded with features, but Quicken was still much easier to use. Where Microsoft Money was an engineering centric product, Quicken was a customer centric product. Intuit held off the Microsoft assault, and Quicken remained the market leader with 88 percent of the market, while Money continued to struggle.[9] Intuit's tireless focus on the customer and its efforts to cultivate relationships with its retailers paid off. While Microsoft flattened other competitors, Intuit continued to thrive.

As the company grew, Intuit added 50 full-time salespeople to manage the relationships with its retail partners. The Intuit sales reps regularly visit stores, give training to the sales staff, and provide information on the company's products, including Quicken, QuickBooks, and

TurboTax.[10] This is a natural extension of the National Sales Tour, and unlike many software companies that hire third-party firms to represent them, Intuit knows all too well how valuable these relationships with retailers are.

Put the Franchisees in Charge

One historically rocky partnership is the love-hate relationship between franchisers and franchisees. In reality, neither can exist without the other, and each benefits from the other's success (usually). One of the biggest and most emotional complaints franchisees have is that they have to pay a percentage of their sales to a central ad fund. The ad fund promotes the entire organization, and each individual franchisee benefits—in theory, at least. Problems arise when franchisees don't agree with the marketing plan, don't like the media breakdown, or they just plain don't like the ads.

When Fred DeLuca started franchising at Subway, the advertising became a source of friction with the franchisees almost from the outset. "At first we planned all the advertising. That's what we did before we had franchisees, so we just kept doing it. Except it triggered a lot of unhappiness. 'Why did you choose this radio station? Why did you run that ad?'" To counter the barrage of criticism, he created a board of directors comprised entirely of franchisees and put them in charge of the ad fund. When they're in charge, decisions are a lot harder to criticize. "For years after I did this, I was told it was the dumbest move anybody could make. "People said franchisees couldn't possibly make the right kind of advertising decisions; that's something that has to be left to the professionals."[11] The friction stopped and the franchisees felt like they were part of the plan.

Ron Joyce took it a step further at Tim Hortons. He created an advisory committee of franchisees, not only to oversee the ad fund, but also to deal with all the operational issues concerning the company. His philosophy was simple: what better people to have involved in making decisions affecting the company than those who are closest to the customer? He brought representatives in from across the country, even paying them to come. They, in turn, represented the store owners in Atlantic Canada or Ontario or British Columbia, so the communications with the owners and the company became very good. They discussed new menu items, new store locations, store design, and any other operational issues. The franchisees worked in the stores on a daily basis and were much closer to the customers—and the problems—than anybody in headquarters.

Instead of seeing himself as the authority and imposing his will on the franchisees, Ron had a completely different view of the relationship. "I always perceived my customer as the franchisee rather than the consumer," Ron said. "The dedication was to ensure you got the proper people, and to make sure that they were profitable, and stick with them very closely to ensure their profitability. That is just good common sense."[12]

And problems did come up. Instead of trying to bury problems or pass the blame, they'd discuss them and look for solutions together. "We sat down and we just lay everything out on the table," Ron said. "They'd come to a meeting and they'd have complaints from an anonymous store owner. How do you address that? We treated it as a very positive thing. We had to make money. We've got to work together."

The advisory committee worked well on a number of fronts. It provided a forum to exchange suggestions and ideas for improving the stores, which would make everyone more money. It also gave store owners a venue to address problems, but in an atmosphere that was positive and productive. When Tim Hortons periodically added new menu items, some store owners would resist the change if it meant they had to buy new equipment. Where a demand issued from headquarters would cause resentment, the advisory board created an open forum that accomplished the same thing in a much more productive manner. The key was creating an environment where Tim Hortons treated franchisees as true partners, and they both won together.

It's Not a Good Deal Unless Both Sides Win

Disney learned an expensive lesson when its partnership with Pixar came up for renewal. When Pixar and Disney teamed up in an agreement to develop three animated films, it was a win for both sides. Pixar was still a small, struggling studio at the time, and the partnership offered instant access to Disney's global distribution network. Disney, in turn, got a 50 percent split from Pixar's movies with virtually no risk. It was the first time Disney turned to an outside studio for an entire movie—screenplay, directing, staging, filming, editing, and post-production. Disney retained licensing rights, and signed deals for spin-off toys and a promotional campaign at Burger King.[13]

The breakout hit *Toy Story*, four years in the making, launched Pixar into prime time. By the time *Toy Story* was released, Pixar had grown from a tiny production lab to a full-fledged studio. Disney and Pixar extended the contract to five films, and with each new movie it released, Pixar gained more respect and more financial clout. *Toy Story* brought in $192 million. Pixar's next three movies—*A Bug's Life, Toy Story 2*, and *Monsters Inc.*—each brought in more than its predecessor. By the end of the decade, Pixar was one of the most consistently profitable studios in Hollywood.[14] That's where the problem with Disney began.

Although the original agreement didn't include any sequels, Pixar agreed to make *Toy Story 2* at Disney's suggestion as a direct-to-video sequel to save time and money. As the project evolved, Pixar CEO Steve Jobs saw its creative and financial potential as a major movie to be released in theaters. Although Disney CEO Michael Eisner resisted, Steve stood his ground. His persistence paid off—*Toy Story 2* became a windfall for Disney, grossing $245 million in the United States. When they started planning for *Toy Story 3*, Pixar was adamant that it be counted as part of the five-film deal. Disney insisted that it wasn't. Despite the fact he initially resisted plans to release *Toy Story 2*—and that Pixar's persistence unexpectedly enriched Disney—the Disney chief wouldn't budge. He refused to compromise and insisted on sticking to the letter of the contract, publicly bragging about the leverage he had over Pixar.[15]

While Pixar's star was rising, Disney's was on the decline. With a series of disappointments such as *Treasure Planet* and *Brother Bear*, Disney relied on Pixar to boost its bottom line. Meanwhile, Pixar continued its hitting streak with *Finding Nemo*, a runaway success that brought in more than $844 million at the box office worldwide.[16] For a small, struggling studio, giving 50 percent of the profit on each movie to Disney in return for a global distribution machine was a great deal. After Pixar's first five movies generated more than $2.5 billion at the box office,[17] the nature of the relationship changed. Pixar had become a respected studio in its own right, and the company had $300 million in the bank and no debt. Lehman Brothers analysts estimate that 45 percent of the operating income in Disney's film studio between 2000 and 2005 would come from Pixar movies—more than $1.1 billion.[18]

Pixar no longer needed Disney, but Disney needed Pixar. Given the changing dynamic in the relationship, it didn't make sense from Pixar's vantage point to do all the work and still share half the profits with Disney. Even more galling was the fact that Disney didn't treat Pixar as an equal in the partnership. Although the relationship and the circumstances changed, Michael Eisner didn't have the flexibility to change with it, and he continued to insist on his interpretation of the original deal to the letter. And while that interpretation was good for Disney, it wasn't good for Pixar. In shoving *Toy Story 3* down Pixar's throat—and then publicly bragging about it—Michael won the battle and lost the war. Pixar later announced it would not renew the agreement, and the windfall Disney experienced from Pixar evaporated.

There's More to Life Than a Lower Price

If your goal is to pound your vendors into submission, you may get what General Motors Vice-Chairman Bob Lutz calls "malicious obedience." In his book *GUTS!*, Bob describes the first turnaround at Chrysler, where he took a cue from a Honda study and began to source from fewer "supplier-partners." Instead of making multiple suppliers compete for an order, essentially killing each other on price for every order, Chrysler reduced the number of suppliers and made the business "theirs to lose" instead of "theirs to beg for." Before that, they'd convinced themselves that having more suppliers undercutting each other was maximizing efficiency—a system that led suppliers to do exactly what was called for and absolutely nothing more. Years later, CEOs of several suppliers confided to him, "You know, Bob, we could have given you that part for half the price if only your people had been willing to change their design just a little bit."[19]

As Lou Pritchett points out, "Put the squeeze on your suppliers, and you're liable to wake up one day and wonder why your packages are falling apart, why the ends are coming unglued, why your toothpaste tastes like—well, like something you wouldn't voluntarily put in your mouth. You have to be as interested in their survival as they are in your survival; you have to be extensions of each other's company."[20]

Mutually Beneficial Relationships

"I don't like the idea of ever having suppliers who are profit maximizers," former Harley-Davidson CEO Rich Teerlink said. "Anyone who is a profit maximizer doesn't care about mutually beneficial relationships." Instead of pounding your suppliers into submission in search of the lowest price, you may save more money in the long run by working closely with them instead of against them. By working together, Procter & Gamble and Wal-Mart both saved money, improved efficiency, and increased profits.

Disney continued to act like it was holding all the cards in its relationship with Pixar, although in fact, that wasn't true anymore. By dictating terms and imposing their will, Disney won the battle and lost the war. On the flip side, Intuit went out of its way to work closely with its distribution partners, and it went to great lengths to cultivate those relationships. Ron Joyce at Tim Hortons and Fred DeLuca at Subway both bent over backward to get their franchisees involved in the decision-making process. While they had bumps along the way, giving their franchisees authority over key parts of the operation were instrumental in each chain's success.

If a partnership only makes sense for one of the parties, it's destined to fail. That's true whether it's a strategic partnership, a supplier-customer relationship, or even a franchisee relationship. Like employees, business partners want to be treated with respect. If it's going to work, the relationship has to be a win for both sides. Nurturing those relationships can pay big dividends; taking them for granted will eventually come back to bite you.

Chapter 16

Make the Mission Come Alive

In 1960, Earl Bakken was in serious trouble. Three years after he invented the world's first wearable, battery-powered pacemaker, his small Minneapolis start-up was trying to introduce the implantable pacemaker. Sales were rising rapidly but so were expenses, and cash was leaving the company faster than it was coming in. Even though their product was a success, the company was flat broke. Like countless other entrepreneurs before and after him, Earl visited local bankers trying to get a line of credit. Every one of them turned him down. Undaunted, he tried a different tactic, commissioning a market research study to demonstrate the potential for the pacemaker. The results weren't what he expected and his plan backfired. The study predicted that the maximum number of devices to be implanted through all history would be less than 10,000. Needless to say, things weren't looking good.

A fellow board member, Tom Holloran, suggested to Earl that what was lacking was a statement of his purpose. Following this advice, Earl sat down and wrote a mission statement for the company. Keep in mind that Earl wrote the mission not when things were going well, but when things were at their worst. Earl took the mission statement to a local venture capitalist and made his case, and he eventually got his funding. The mission statement he wrote became the guiding principle of his young company, and it helped chart the course in the following years as the company grew. Earl's company, Medtronic, not only survived, but became a leader in the medical industry, growing to more than $6 billion in sales and $30 billion in market value.

Bill George, who joined the company as president after running Honeywell and Litton, believes Medtronic's secret to success is its over-riding sense of purpose at all levels of the company. "Medtronic is very much a mission-driven company, and we spend a great deal of time with employees—from people doing the work on production lines to designers to salespeople—talking about the mission; the values of quality, service, and integrity; and having an open system of communication so if there's any quality problem, those can surface to the top of the organization as quickly as possible."[1]

As Bill explains, "The first statement is really the mission statement. The succeeding five statements describe the values we use to carry out our mission. The significant thing about the Medtronic mission statement is that not one word has been changed since Earl originally wrote it in 1960."

Make It Real

Like many other companies, Medtronic has the mission statement in prominent locations throughout the company. They also have pictures of their patients lining the hallways to remind everyone who their customers are. They take it much further, though, using a variety of programs to make sure the mission really hits home for every employee.

The most important event of the year at Medtronic is the annual holiday program, a tradition the company has observed for more than 40 years. Each December, the company invites six patients and their doctors to come to Medtronic and tell their personal stories to Medtronic employees. With 1,500 people packed into the auditorium and thousands more around the world watching by videoconference, the doctors and their patients explain how Medtronic's artificial hearts, pacemakers, and other products have changed or saved their lives. "We have patients who come in who would be dead if it wasn't for us," one employee said. "I mean, they sit right up there and they tell us what their lives are like. You don't walk away from them not feeling anything."[2]

The night before Bill's first Medtronic holiday program, Earl told him to keep a lookout for a young 18-year-old boy named T.J. Flack, who had suffered from cerebral palsy since birth. In front of the Medtronic employees, T.J. told the story of what his life had been like for his first 17 years. He had major surgery every June, he was in a body cast all summer, and then his spasticity would return during the rest of the year. At age 16, he refused further surgery and his body became increasingly rigid. At 18, T.J. received one of the first clinical treatments of the drug Baclofen, used in conjunction with the Medtronic SynchroMed programmable drug pump.

T.J.'s life had changed dramatically. He could get out of bed in the morning, dress himself, and climb five flights of stairs to his mainstream school. His speech improved, and he even played wheelchair basketball. Bill saw in T.J. a lot of characteristics of his own son, who was also 18 years old, but who was completely healthy. As he listened to T.J.'s story, he felt tears come to his eyes. "At first, I was a bit embarrassed until I looked at the executive sitting next to me, who was also crying."

Ironically, when Bill first joined Medtronic, the manager of new ventures told him the Executive Committee had decided to sell the drug pump business because it was losing so much money. Fortunately, no one showed up to buy it in the intervening six months before T.J.'s presentation. After listening to T.J. tell his story, Bill got a group of people together and decided to cancel the sale and reorganize the division. From a purely financial point of view, selling or closing the money-losing division would have made sense. But in light of their mission—specifically keeping in mind people like T.J.—that wasn't even an option for Bill. Instead of ditching the division, they cut the administrative expenses, increased R&D, and put it under the neurological group. The drug pump business quickly became profitable, and shortly thereafter it became Medtronic's fastest growing business.

T.J. went on to graduate from college, get married, and get a job in the communications industry. Long after that holiday program, he was still an inspiration for Bill. "As one of our executives said, every Medtronic employee has a defining moment when the mission goes from being an intellectual concept to a passion in your heart. Meeting T.J. Flack was my defining moment."

Make It Personal

Another Medtronic tradition Earl started early on to reinforce the mission was having the CEO personally greet every new employee, explain the mission to them, and give them a medallion with the company's mission on it. These medallion ceremonies continued as the company grew, and Earl traveled all over the world to meet new employees. At the medallion ceremony Earl would go over the founding, and the mission, word by word, explaining what it means to him. Then he would call up each employee individually and give them a medallion with "the rising man," symbolic of the mission, and ask them to make a commitment to the Medtronic mission: "Put this medallion at your workplace and remember why you're here: not just to make money for yourself or the company, but to help restore people to full life and health."

When Bill George joined Medtronic, he helped Earl with the medallion ceremonies. When he later took over as CEO, he continued the tradition, often with Earl accompanying him, personally meeting every new employee. In one quarter, Bill went to Europe four times for medallion ceremonies in France, Germany, Spain, and the UK. After succeeding Bill as CEO, Art Collins carried on the tradition. As Bill explains, it's kind of like joining a club, because the medallions can only be given to Medtronic employees.

As you can imagine, personally meeting every new employee in a company of 28,000 requires a continual commitment and a huge investment of time. Some people might argue that the CEO has more important things to do than to greet every new employee and talk about the mission. The leaders at Medtronic disagree. They believe that this investment of time to continually reinforce the mission is a crucial part of the company's success. As Bill points out, Medtronic is dealing with life and death every day. "Every time you produce a thousand heart valves or a thousand pacemakers, there is a good chance someone is going to die if that product fails. That's why it's so important that everyone understand the consequences and take responsibility for it."

At one medallion ceremony in Lausanne, Switzerland, Medtronic's European team arranged for four patients and their physicians to tell their stories. One of them was a big Swiss farmer with Parkinson's disease who suffered from the tremors. His doctor asked him to demonstrate how the tremor abated by using a Medtronic device. Then the doctor asked him to shut the device off, and immediately the tremors returned. When he turned the device back on, the tremors stopped immediately. "A loud gasp went up from the employees in the audience," Bill recalls. "In that instant, our 150 new Swiss employees 'got it.' They knew why the quality of their pacemakers, defibrillators, and stimulators had to be perfect and what they were working for."[3]

"A mission is not about a code of conduct, rules, systems, and procedures. It is about having a sense of purpose and a set of values that guide our everyday actions," Bill said.[4] "It sounds philosophical, but that's the way it actually works. I don't believe you motivate people strictly by money. They've got to be inspired by the work they're doing."

Get People Excited About What You're Doing

You don't have to be making a life-or-death product to have the vision of the company inspire your employees. As Bill George points out, Hewlett-Packard had a driving sense of mission for 40 years with the "HP way." "Hewlett-Packard's kind of lost it now, but for 40 years the 'HP way' was the driving factor of that whole company. They were not in a life-and-death business, but every employee knew the HP way, and they were committed to it. They knew Bill Hewlett and Dave Packard. They certainly knew a lot of folklore and company stories about them." Having a sense of purpose is just as important in big companies as in small, regardless of your industry.

Sheldon Laube has a similar perspective. The former CTO of USWeb and Novell, Sheldon founded CenterBeam to run the back-office information technology (IT) departments for other companies—a decidedly unglamorous area of IT. "Being able to inspire isn't important just for people who run high-tech start-ups," Sheldon explains. "Every leader has to do that, whether you're the CEO of the country or the CEO of a small business."[5]

Sheldon was talking to someone who asked, "Aren't you bored? You do the really boring stuff in IT, making PCs work and running networks and stuff like that. How do you get excited about that?" Sheldon's answer was as simple as it is passionate: "This is a problem that faces millions of people every day. Their computers frustrate them! That's a big deal. It might not be very sexy, but boy our customers love what we do for them."

Even though he's in a completely different industry, Sheldon reiterates the same theme as Bill George. You've got to believe in what you're doing and you have to be able to communicate that to people. "It doesn't matter how mundane what you do is. You don't have to be inventing the cure for cancer," Sheldon said. "You have to be able to communicate that it's really a big deal. Then you have to motivate each person and let them know that their job is important, and that they are an integral piece of making this work."[6]

Find Your Focus

Once you've defined your mission and communicated it throughout the organization, the next thing you need to do is continually reinforce it. One way to do that is to develop a framework or benchmark you measure everything against. When Richard Tait first dreamed up Cranium, his idea was to invent a game that was competitive and fun, but that also gave everyone a chance to shine in front of their family and friends. "We really look at the lifestyle moments that we're trying to capture and see how we can bring them to life and celebrate them in a game experience," Richard explains. For example, Cranium Kadoo, the kids game, is built around moments where kids will stand in front of their parents and say, "Mommy, Daddy, look what I can do!" "We wanted to capture that moment and give parents and their kids a chance to experience it maybe 20 times in a 30-minute play experience."[7]

"The soul of this company is to lighten and enlighten people's lives," Richard says. To do that, Cranium strives to give them smart, fun play experiences. To keep from straying from its mission, Cranium came up with a framework it calls CHIFF—Clever, High quality, Innovative, Friendly, and Fun. They continually ask themselves, "Does it really meet the internal bar that we have?"

Every card in every game has to pass the test, but the CHIFF checklist goes far beyond developing moments for the game. Every decision in the company—from marketing to product development to finance—goes through the CHIFF checklist to make sure that it really stays true to the Cranium brand. If an idea is friendly and fun, but not innovative and clever, it doesn't pass muster. If something is clever, but not particularly fun, it doesn't fly either. By using this simple checklist, everyone in the company has a simple barometer to make sure they don't stray off the path. "Every single person that touches Cranium is touched with a CHIFF brush," Richard says. This simple litmus test helps them stay true to their vision and strengthen their brand.

Don't Stray off the Path

Having a strong vision isn't enough. You also have to constantly remind everyone—including yourself—why you're there. If you don't clearly define that vision, it's easy to lose direction and stray off the path. John Peterman started his company on the strength of a duster coat he found in Jackson Hole, Wyoming. When he wore the coat, people gave him approving glances and reacted to him in a different way. The duster conjured up romantic notions of rugged adventures in faraway places. It implied the wearer was on an intellectual or emotional journey, and, with that, evoked a sense of wonder. He felt transformed when he wore it. He realized that if he could find other products that captured this feeling, people would pay for it.

In the fall of 1988, the first J. Peterman Company *Owner's Manual* catalog with black-and-white drawings accompanied by romantic descriptions was released—it had a grand total of seven items in it. "There wasn't a huge amount of strategizing involved in creating the J. Peterman catalog business," said John, the founder of the company bearing his name. "It was intuitive, it fit, it felt right."

The next spring, the first color catalog went out. Their staff at the time consisted of three full-time people and four part-timers, and John couldn't even afford to take a salary. By 1989, the young company did $4.8 million in sales, and increased to $19.8 million in 1990. The staff increased to 80 people, all working well together toward a common, if unstated, goal. The future looked bright.

Although he never stopped to write down a mission statement, he decided later that the spirit of the company was captured in six words— unique, authentic, romantic, journey, wondrous, and excellent. The first J. Peterman products were all that. Until 1996, the theory of his business was in his head. Together with his cofounder and creative director, John always found time to make sure that it was also in the heads of everyone else on the staff. As the company grew, though, this shared vision started to slip. To overcome the flat revenue growth, they laid the plans for a retail expansion and quickly recruited a lot more people. As the pace of the business increased, something got lost along the way. "In the face of success and rapid growth, it's easy to assume that people joining the team know what the game is," John said. "Failing to make sure that everyone knows what you stand for and why—that can come right back and ambush you much sooner than you realize."[8]

In 1995, J. Peterman became a character on *Seinfeld*, which was then the number-one television show in the country. Actor John O'Hurley, portraying J. Peterman, was Elaine's boss on the show. Some people said later that John missed a great opportunity to take advantage of the publicity the show offered, but he didn't think so. Commercializing it didn't feel right. "We did put an Elaine Bennis suit into our catalog, mostly as a way of winking at our customers. But I regret doing that. It was one of those little decisions that was slightly off point for our brand." Even though it sold moderately well, he realized later that it was a step in the wrong direction. "It may have been an excellent suit, but it did not embody any of the other elements. It was not romantic or wondrous. It represented no sort of journey."[9]

The first *Seinfeld* appearance also marked the beginning of the end for J. Peterman. The same month there was a substantial increase in the cost of postage and paper, two of the catalog company's biggest expenses. J. Peterman had a significant loss that year. The company managed to break even the following year, mainly by cutting back on advertising and mailing fewer catalogs to more profitable customers. The pressure to grow from their venture capital investors increased, though, and the company strayed further from that original vision.

What they should have done, John realized later, was cut back on the number of products they offered. "The more-is-better theory didn't work for us in practice. The more items we offered, whether through the catalogs or the stores, the less special—the less 'Peterman'—each new item became." There was another problem that went hand-in-hand with the first. The more products they added, the more staff they needed to support the increasing product line. They also needed new business systems to support the increased staff and burgeoning product line. "It was too much change at once, and it was a recipe for disaster."

The investors were demanding growth, and to get that growth, they wanted John to bring in outside talent. At first glance, this didn't seem to be an unreasonable request. But the outside managers they brought in didn't have time to get their feet on the ground. "We didn't have time to keep reinforcing what we assumed was a rock-solid culture. And so the new team didn't have time to gel. There was friction; there was confusion." Little by little, John was losing control, even as they were picking up speed. As the company grew in a desperate race to outrun its problems, they strayed off the path and went deeper and deeper into the woods. In 1999, the J. Peterman Company filed for bankruptcy.

Looking back, John is philosophical. "When we matched our products with those six words, we were successful," John recalls. "When we strayed from the six words, we faltered. Toward the end of the company, we were developing 2,000 new products a year. There is just no way to generate 2,000 products that are truly romantic, unique, and authentic."[10]

Stay True to Your Vision

Even when you believe in the vision, you'll often run into opposition from people who don't share your view; especially if it involves changing direction. If you believe in it, don't let anyone else rain on your parade. In the early 1980s, Starbucks was a small Seattle retailer of whole coffee beans, grinders, and coffee-makers. The only way to drink Starbucks coffee at the time was to buy the beans, take them home, and grind them yourself. Howard Schultz had been the company's vice president of marketing for a year when he went to Italy for a conference. While he was there, he was captivated by the charm and romance of the neighborhood espresso bars.

As he wandered around the streets of Rome, he had a revelation; the connection to the people who loved coffee didn't have to take place only in their homes, where they ground and brewed whole-bean coffee. "Starbucks had completely missed the point—completely missed it," Howard said. "What we had to do was unlock the romance and mystery of coffee, firsthand, in coffee bars. The Italians understood the personal relationship that people could have to coffee, its social aspect. I couldn't believe that Starbucks was in the coffee business, yet was overlooking so central an element in it."[11]

Howard didn't spot the coffee trend in the United States—he invented it. "The Italians had turned the drinking of coffee into a symphony, and it felt right. Starbucks was playing in the same hall, but we were playing without a string section." He brought that vision and excitement back to Seattle, but was unable to convince the Starbucks owners the company should change direction. He stayed true to his dream, ultimately leaving Starbucks to open his own coffee bars, which he named Il Giornaio. His idea was to give people a little escape during their day. Although they might not be able to take a vacation, they could have a refuge for a few minutes with a steaming cup of coffee. Even though coffee was a commodity, Howard believed he could weave a sense of romance and community around it. "We would rediscover the mystique and charm that had swirled around coffee through the centuries. We would enchant customers with an atmosphere of sophistication and style and knowledge."

He wasn't just selling coffee by the cup. Like John Peterman, he was selling charm and romance. When the Starbucks owners later decided to sell the company, Howard jumped at the chance and bought it, and the rest is history. "Without the romance of Italian espresso, Starbucks would still be what it once was, a beloved local coffee bean company."[12]

Don't Let the Bean Counters Make Policy Decisions

A strong accounting department is an essential element of any enterprise, but you have to remember that accountants are not paid to be visionaries. Their job is to keep tight control of expenses. As such, their viewpoint is 180 degrees off from most other people who are trying to move the company ahead. That's okay—it's even a good thing—as long as you don't let them get out of control.

Imagine this scenario: Howard Schultz is about to open his first neighborhood coffee bar in Seattle, and his accountant says, "You're spending too much money on lights and décor. Let's cut the expenses." Sure, he could have opened more stores for less money. He also could have sold coffee cheaper. But that wasn't what Starbucks was all about. Howard wanted to enchant customers with style and sophistication, and he couldn't do that by cutting corners on the store build-out. The charm and ambience that makes Starbucks so unique would have been lost, and the company would never have become what it is today. Like the "good" financial decision to sell the money-losing drug pump unit at Medtronic, looking at it strictly in financial terms doesn't help you stay true to your mission. Let the accountants do their job, but don't let them do yours.

Why Are You Really Here?

Ely Callaway's mission wasn't to sell more golf clubs than anyone else. That's what eventually happened, but that was a result—not a goal. His mission was to make the game of golf more enjoyable for the average player. Everything the company did was centered around that goal, from making irons to putters to golf balls—even making Little Big Bertha clubs for kids. David Neeleman's mission when he started JetBlue was to bring humanity back to air travel. JetBlue has done exactly that, from putting DirecTV in every seat to charging employees with "doing the right thing" for customers. The success that both companies had in the marketplace was a direct result of following that vision.

Management guru Jeffrey Garten, dean of the Yale School of Management, calls it finding true north. As Garten explains in his book *Mind of the CEO*, it's important for the leader to have a strong compass in the stormy seas of business. With people changing jobs faster, customers shopping around more, and shareholders churning their portfolios, Garten argues that CEOs who can provide a strong anchor are more important than ever.[13]

This is true well beyond the executive suite, though. Leaders at all levels need that sense of mission, the overriding principles to act as the compass in the storm. It goes beyond corporate strategy and permeates down to the smallest decision. It comes shining through in countless ways, and its impact reverberates throughout the organization. Sharing a sense of direction and purpose will help keep every decision—both large and small—on track.

After a particularly bad snowstorm in the Northeast, JetBlue sent travel vouchers to thousands of customers who had been stranded when the airports shut down. Even though the delay was caused by weather, they felt they could have handled things better and they apologized to their customers. That small move cost the company several million dollars. But were they staying true to their mission? Absolutely. Did that decision follow their vision of returning humanity to air travel? Definitely. And even though it cost them money in the short run, it cemented the loyalty of their customers in the long run.

Inspiration Doesn't Happen on Its Own

Mission statements have become a popular management tool in recent years. Unfortunately, most companies approach it like another management fad and it rarely has the desired impact throughout the organization. Writing a mission statement simply isn't enough. Most likely, it will be greeted with a yawn at the lower levels of the organization. In order to get people excited about it, they need to understand why they're really there. Making money isn't enough. People want to believe in what they're doing.

One of the biggest problems a company faces is staying true to its guiding principles as the company grows. With the constant pressure cooker of investor expectations, competitive threats, and a changing workforce, you have to juggle a lot of competing demands. As your business grows, adding employees dilutes the culture of veterans on the staff. With so many constituencies to please, it's hard to keep everyone moving in the same direction. In good times and bad, you have to constantly reinforce those values to remind everyone why you're there in the first place.

Some people will argue that it's easy to make sure everyone understands and believes in the mission in a small company, but that it's not practical—or even possible—to do so in a larger organization. Sure, you can print mission statements on the back of business cards and hang posters in the conference room, but how effective is that in conveying the ideals and vision behind the company? Communicating these ideals to a larger group is more challenging, but it's certainly not impossible. Medtronic has proven that. That's not to say that it's easy. It does require constant reinforcement and commitment from the top. As Medtronic has proven, the rewards are great if that sense of purpose is shared throughout the company. And as J. Peterman demonstrated, the risks are high when you lose that sense of purpose and stray off the path.

When J. Peterman stopped focusing on its six values—unique, authentic, romantic, journey, wondrous, and excellent—the company started to lose direction. Trying to outrun its problems, the company focused on growth, and added more people and more products—as well as new systems to support them—and lost track of the ideals that made the company unique in the first place. It's easy to get so caught up in making your numbers, closing the next sale, and dealing with the hectic pace of day-to-day life that you lose sight of your original vision.

A mission isn't just a piece of paper on the wall of the conference room. It's the very essence of the company—the reason you're in business. What are you all about? You're not there just to make money, or to increase "shareholder value." Those things happen if you're true to your mission and if everyone in the company shares that sense of purpose. Vision isn't just writing down the corporate mission and sending out a memo. It's a living, breathing thing, and it has to be constantly reinforced. As Marc Allen writes in *Visionary Business*, "Money is the lifeblood of the business, but the business has to have a higher purpose to survive and thrive."[14]

Chapter 17

Keep It Special

In an era of managing quarterly earnings and making decisions based on the stock price, doing the right thing often takes second place to economic expediency. Many companies go to great lengths to maximize profits—even at the expense of their customers or employees—when they would do better to focus on preserving the value of their brand. All the mission statements and strategic planning in the world won't do a bit of good if you don't deliver a quality product or service.

What is it that makes your company special? It's not necessarily the product. Over time, products come and go as the company moves on. What makes your company special are the experience, the emotion, and the feelings it conveys to your customers. At JOE BOXER, Bill Sweedler tests every idea against the "DNA of the brand." At Cranium, Richard Tait evaluates every game question, product idea, and marketing plan to make sure it meets the CHIFF test (Clever, High quality, Innovative, Friendly, and Fun).

Over time, every company develops a unique identity that shapes the way customers respond in the marketplace. If you focus only on the bottom line, you may be tempted to cut corners when it comes to quality. Instead of focusing on ways to increase sales and make more money, don't overlook something just as important—what can you do to keep your company special?

A Blue Attitude

As part of his mission to bring humanity back to air travel, David Neeleman rewrote the rules of the airline industry. Customer response to JetBlue was so strong that established carriers such as United and Delta launched their own low fare airlines—Ted and Song—in an effort to capture some of JetBlue's magic.

So what makes JetBlue so special? Everything from the smallest details—blue potato chips to the seatback guide to "Airplane yoga: or how to look like a real weirdo to your fellow passengers"—all contribute to a feeling that this airline is different. Even the organization of the company is different—100 percent of JetBlue's call-center employees work from home. Who wouldn't be happy with flexible hours and no commute?

Sure, they have brand-new planes with leather seats and personal video screens with DirecTV in every seatback, but any airline could have done that. While those advantages gave the company a competitive edge, they're only temporary. After all, there is nothing stopping other airlines from doing the same thing. Remember the first rental car company to use wireless check-in so you don't have to wait in line to turn in your car? Now they all do it. A short-term competitive edge doesn't make a long-term sustainable advantage.

While other airlines may copy parts of JetBlue's formula, what really sets JetBlue apart is its attitude. That filters down from the top, beginning with a CEO who works at least one flight a week, loading bags, taking tickets, and cleaning the airplanes. The focus isn't on rules, but on doing what's right for the customer. That's all part of the ultrahip personality JetBlue established, and that's the company's most valuable asset. Every decision, large and small, affects the customers' perceptions. By rewriting the book on what airlines are all about, David Neeleman set a new standard for air travel and raised the bar for his competition.

Always Give Them More Than They Expect

Dave Gold didn't invent discounting, but he certainly put a new spin on it. When he was working in his family liquor store, he noticed that items sold a lot faster if they were marked 99 cents instead of $1.02.

For 20 years he kicked around his idea of opening a store where everything would sell for 99 cents. One day Dave was at lunch with his wife and an old friend, and he brought up the idea of a 99 cent store one time too many. His friend, who had spotted a vacant store that morning said, "Here's a location, damn it. Open up there!" He did just that. Putting his money where his mouth was, Dave opened the first 99 Cents Only store in 1972 when he was 50 years old. Since then, he's never looked back. Sticking to the same formula, he opened 200 stores in the next 20 years and built a billion-dollar business by giving people more than they expect.

From the outset, Dave had a vision that his stores would be sparkling. People don't expect much for 99 cents, and he wanted to impress his customers. There are now a host of dollar store knockoffs that have copied Dave, and most have cluttered stores filled with cheap merchandise in disarray. In many cases, dollar stores sell things nobody wants—hence the end of its retail journey at a bargain store that sells discarded merchandise. Not so in Dave's stores; 99 Cent Only stores are pristine, with rows after row of neatly stacked brand-name products that look almost like a work of art. The cleanliness and merchandising inside his stores would make Target proud. In fact, a 9 × 7–foot photo of the inside of a 99 Cents Only store by famed photographer Andreas Gursky is on display at the Metropolitan Museum of Art. It only takes about one minute to realize that it is no ordinary discount store.

First-time visitors walk in with low expectations. After seeing it, their first reaction is "wow!" It's hard not to be impressed with how neat, clean, and well organized everything is. Repeat customers know they're going to get a great experience, even if they don't know exactly what it will be. Even though the company cut its teeth on close-outs and buying unsold inventory from other companies, 55 percent of the merchandise is from big, brand-name manufacturers. You'll find brand-name products from makers such as Heinz, Gerber, Kraft, Yoplait, Ivory Liquid, Ghirardelli, and Häagen-Dazs in a store the size of a small supermarket. The other 45 percent is the treasure hunt. That doesn't mean it's the no-name knickknacks that people rarely have reason to buy. While the dollar knockoffs dedicate 45 percent of their inventory to such items, they make up less then 2 percent of the inventory at 99 Cents Only.[1]

A New Spin on Value

When Jill Birnbaum, a buyer for 99 Cents Only, was offered a deal on marker sets from an upscale manufacturer for 40 cents, she thought the price was too high. When she went home that night, she saw her roommate using the same markers, but she had paid $9.99. Jill bought the whole lot, and they quickly sold at 99 cents.[2] That's part of the anticipation and discovery a trip to 99 Cents Only brings. Customers leave feeling they've gotten more than their money's worth. And they have.

When 99 Cents Only started stocking wine, customers were skeptical and it didn't sell well. After all, when you buy a bottle of wine for 99 cents, you expect it to taste like something you'd use to clean your floor. Then the *LA Times* ran a story rating the best wines for less than $5, with the categories ranging from "pour down the drain" and "serve your enemies" on the low end to top ranks such as "good for drinking at home" and "serve with pride." The only wine to get five stars ("serve with pride") was from 99 Cents Only.[3] When the story came out, they sold out all the remaining 17,000 bottles in two hours. They still sell wine (when they can get a good wine at a great price), and newer stores have even added a "fancy gourmet food" section.

One of the most powerful weapons in Dave's arsenal is the uncanny ability to continually surprise and delight his customers. Part of this is by design, such as opening every store a few minutes before the posted hours and closing a few minutes late. "It used to bug me," Dave explained. "I'd go to the department store 10 minutes before they close, and you couldn't get anybody to help you."[4] Little things like this make a difference, and customers appreciate it.

The other part of giving people more than they expect is through focus and execution—delivering high-quality merchandise the people just don't expect to find for 99 cents. Browsing through the store is like going on a treasure hunt. You find so many brand-name products at such outrageously low prices, it's hard to resist stocking up on things you had no intention of buying.

Although that wasn't his intent, he's also built 99 Cents Only into a cultural phenomenon. The Goo Goo Dolls and The Rolling Stones shot videos in his stores, and movie stars such as Richard Gere, Vanna White, and even Martha Stewart have been spotted shopping there. Why pay more if you don't have to?[5]

In 20 years, Dave built 99 Cents Only from one small store near the Los Angeles airport to a sprawling billion-dollar chain marching steadily eastward. Like every other successful business, there are a lot of factors contributing to Dave's success. He takes care of his people, leads by example, and he's very careful about spending money. But the one underlying theme is that over the years, Dave consistently gave his customers much more than they expect, earning the devotion of his loyal customers and the admiration of converted skeptics.

Keep It Real

In the early 1990s, Albert Straus and his sister Vivian faced the very grim possibility of losing their family's dairy farm. Small family dairies were vanishing at an alarming rate, and of the 150 dairies originally in Marin County, California, there were less than 30 left. As the big commercial dairies got bigger, life for the family farms grew increasingly difficult. Albert knew he had to do something different in order to survive.

When someone approached him about making organic milk for ice cream, Albert was intrigued. He had taken courses on it in college at Cal Poly in San Luis Obispo, California, but there was no clear definition of what it meant to be organic. Although the customer gave up on the idea, Albert pursued it.

In 1993, the Straus family farm became the first certified organic dairy west of the Mississippi River. To be certified organic, the dairy went three years without using pesticides, herbicides, or synthetic fertilizers. It didn't use any hormones or antibiotics on the cows, and the feed was all from organic sources.

In 1994, four days after the federal government approved use of the Bovine Growth Hormone (rBST or rBGH), Albert opened the Straus Family Creamery to bottle milk and make dairy products under the family name. While other dairies were becoming larger to get economies of scale, Albert intentionally kept the size of the herd small to maintain the land and the health of the cows.

Albert took it a step further, going to great lengths to use environmentally friendly practices and reduce waste. He invested in cogeneration equipment to capture methane gas from the pond, and the creamery now generates twice as much electricity as it uses. He also recycled water and strictly avoided using chemicals that are detrimental to the environment. By focusing on sustainability, he decreased operating costs and helped the environment at the same time.

In a throwback to an earlier era, the Straus Family Creamery began selling milk in recyclable glass bottles. Because each bottle is reused an average of seven times, it dramatically cut raw materials costs. Although it requires extra work on the part of customers to return or recycle the bottles—and extra work on the part of the creamery to take them back—many customers appreciate the effort the company makes to do the right thing.

In 2003, 10 years after converting to organic, the Straus Family Creamery introduced three flavors of super premium organic ice cream—Raspberry, Dutch Chocolate, and Vanilla Bean. Straus organic ice cream tastes like Häagen-Dazs, but it contains only organic ingredients—no concentrates, gums, or artificial coloring or flavoring. The vanilla is made from real ground vanilla beans, and the raspberry is made with raspberry puree. In fact, Straus ice cream beat Häagen-Dazs 50 percent of the time in blind taste tests, and it quickly became the best-selling new product at Whole Foods Markets.

The family farm that was in jeopardy a decade earlier is thriving, and other local dairies began joining the extended Straus family, converting to organic and supplying the creamery with milk. Straus Family Creamery now supplies organic milk, yogurt, cheese, and super premium ice cream throughout the West Coast to Trader Joe's, Wild Oats, and Whole Foods Markets. Revenues have more than doubled, while operating costs have decreased. By taking the high road, Albert earned a reputation as a leader in sustainable business practices, and the Straus Family Creamery built a strong base of loyal customers who appreciate the company's environmentally responsible practices.

If You're Not Proud of It, Don't Put Your Name on It

A big part of protecting the value of your brand is refusing to cut corners when it comes to quality. As a natural extension of its popular seafood restaurants, Legal Seafoods expanded into shipping fresh seafood nationwide using a specially created container. In doing so, Legal

Seafoods added a new dimension to the business and extended its brand outside the geographic area. After all, considering its position as a seafood company that happens to operate restaurants, the mail-order business made perfect sense. Legal was playing to its strengths.

With the restaurants thriving and the mail-order business off to a strong start, the next step in leveraging the brand was to launch a wholesale operation, providing Legal Seafoods products to local supermarkets, much the same as Krispy Kreme does with doughnuts. The company contracted with suppliers, designed the packaging, and put all the wheels in motion to start wholesaling seafood products, beginning with their signature clam chowder. As the first batch was ready to deliver to the stores, Roger Berkowitz brought the whole operation to a screeching halt. As Roger explains, "It was a perfectly acceptable product—but it didn't taste like our clam chowder."[6]

Even though his decision cost Legal Seafoods a bundle in lost profits—not to mention the time, effort, and resources invested up to that point—Roger never had a doubt that it was the right thing to do. The Legal Seafoods brand was worth far more than the money he lost on the clam chowder.

John Lassiter made the same decision at Pixar near the completion of *Toy Story 2*. Despite the two and a half years invested in the film, the story didn't feel right and the ending wasn't taking shape. Pixar was running out of time. Given the tight production deadline, John knew it would be virtually impossible to rewrite the existing story (it usually takes four years to produce an animated film, and they only had nine months left). Instead of moving ahead when Pixar wasn't happy with the film, the company threw out the script and started all over again, and remade the entire movie in just nine months. If Pixar had pressed on and released a film it wasn't happy with, the film may have tarnished a stellar brand. Instead, *Toy Story 2* went on to become another blockbuster, and Pixar continued its winning streak.[7]

Don't Settle for Less

While many companies go to great lengths to maximize profits, the Boston Beer Company literally pours a million dollars' worth of Samuel Adams beer down the drain every year because it's past the expiration date. Unlike dairy products, there is no safety risk; it's strictly an issue of quality and taste. By destroying old beer, Jim Koch maintains the consistently high quality that sets Samuel Adams beer apart from the crowd.

What many people don't realize is that beer loses its freshness when it's exposed to light or it just gets old. But these factors don't stop other brewing companies from selling it anyway. After all, it's a cash cow and most people can't tell the difference. Although Budweiser started promoting its "born on" date, Jim thinks that's still missing the point. "What good would it do to put the date on a milk carton telling you what day the cow was milked? Do you want to have to figure that out yourself?"[8] From the outset, Samuel Adams beer has always had a "good until" date printed on the label. If it's past the date, he won't let distributors sell it—even though it means lost profits and more work to collect and destroy it.

In addition to destroying beer once it's past the expiration date, the Boston Beer Company takes it a step further, doing 12,000 quality audits on draft beer around the country. Virtually every bar that sells a significant amount of Sam Adams beer on draft gets audited at least twice a year. There are a number of things that can cause problems when draft beer is served in a bar or restaurant: the beer isn't kept cold enough, the lines aren't kept clean, or the air compressors put oxygen into the beer instead of CO_2 or nitrogen.[9]

All Samuel Adams salespeople are trained in tasting, and they show up unannounced, taste the beer, check the lines, inspect the cooler, check temperature, and evaluate the taste. If it doesn't pass muster, they call in a draft technician to identify the problem. If the establishment doesn't correct the problem to their satisfaction, they can't sell it anymore. "We've pulled our beer out of accounts that simply can't serve it right," Jim said.[10]

Although most companies like to believe they're committed to quality, few go to the great lengths the Boston Beer Company does to ensure quality at the point of sale. "If you go into a bar, you don't know whether they're cleaning the lines or keeping the beer cold. That's our job," Jim explained. "If it's Sam Adams, you can be confident that it's the most reliable quality in the beer business." In the long run, that consistent quality is worth every penny.

The Company Is the Product

By giving the customer a great experience and refusing to sacrifice on quality, you can preserve and protect the value of your brand. Dave Gold built 99 Cents Only into a billion-dollar company by consistently giving customers more than they expect. Like Doug Dayton in the early days of Target, customers didn't expect 99 Cents Only to have quality products and attractive merchandising, and he continually surprised them.

In addition to establishing the first organic dairy farm on the West Coast, Albert Straus went to great lengths to use sustainable practices at the Straus Family Creamery, from generating its own electricity to using returnable glass bottles. In the process, he developed a strong following and a sterling reputation that goes far beyond the company's products. Legal Seafoods and the Boston Beer Company both gave away profits rather than take the risk of tarnishing their brands. Similarly, Pixar went back to the drawing board on *Toy Story 2* rather than release a film it wasn't happy with.

At the end of the day, your reputation is your greatest asset. Your company's identity and brand are shaped by every decision you make. Whatever your unique blend of assets are, look for ways you can shine in your customers' eyes. Even if it costs you in short-term profits, your company will be much stronger if you constantly look for ways to preserve and protect the DNA of your brand.

Chapter 18

Take Care of Your People and They'll Take Care of You

W hen Marilyn Carlson Nelson became CEO of Carlson Companies, she took over for her father, a strong-willed entrepreneur who built the travel empire through sheer willpower and ruled with an iron fist. Marilyn put her own stamp on the company, expanding benefits, creating a profit-sharing program, and adding flex-time and a daycare center, along with a series of bonuses tied to growth.[1] You don't often hear the CEO of a global corporation talk about the importance of families, but from Marilyn's perspective, the company is a family of families. "I think you can lead the company with love, but it does have to be tough love," Marilyn explained. "When you have to take a difficult step, you try to take it in the most caring way that you can."[2]

According to Trudy Rautio, president of Carlson Hotels Worldwide, "Marilyn leads from the heart. She has the unique ability to capture your heart first and then you will move mountains to achieve her objectives."[3]

Dave Gold has the same perspective. Like Marilyn, he treats his employees the same way he treats his customers and vendors—with generosity and respect. While it's not unusual to hear about founders and early employees of successful companies striking riches, at 99 Cents Only, the truck drivers, warehouse workers, and retail sales staff are also big winners. In addition to giving health insurance to everyone, Dave gives all employees, including part-time workers, stock options.

With the stock splitting five times in nine years after its IPO, 99 Cents Only employees have plenty of reasons to be happy. By treating his employees right, Dave created a vibrant place to work and laid the foundation for a highly successful company.

When leaders build a strong culture based on respect for their employees combined with a real sense of purpose, people are happy to come to work—and it shows. When employees believe they are doing something important, they're challenged, and they feel appreciated by the company, it creates an uplifting effect throughout the organization. Not only do they treat customers better, but they do their jobs better.

As Home Depot cofounder Arthur Blank summed it up, "The core belief that we have is that if our associates don't feel like we care for them, they're not going to care for the customers in our stores."[4]

A Kid-Friendly Furniture Company

You don't have to be a billion-dollar company to create an employee-friendly environment. With $40 million in sales, the Mitchell Gold Furniture Company was selling furniture to retailers such as Crate & Barrel, Pottery Barn, and Restoration Hardware, as well as catalogs such as Neiman Marcus and L.L. Bean. The company's award-winning contemporary furniture was even selling in Europe and Asia. Sales were strong, the company was making money, and life was good.

Then Mitchell Gold got an unusual idea. He noticed that around 4 o'clock every day, he was losing many of his employees. People with kids stopped focusing on work and started worrying about picking up their kids from daycare on time. Many daycare centers fine parents if they're late picking up kids, and given the choice of picking up their kids or finishing a project at work, it wasn't hard to guess where their priorities were. Even though he didn't have kids, he realized childcare was very stressful for the parents, and the stress was affecting the company.

When the company was expanding its facilities and building a new factory, Mitchell suggested to his partner Bob that they also add a daycare facility. His idea was simple—make life a little better for his employees who had children. Adding on-site childcare would remove the anxiety or worry for a child in a remote facility.

Mitchell and Bob immediately ran into opposition from their attorney, accountant, and insurance company—all of whom were worried about liability. Mitchell knew of another company that ran an on-site daycare center, so he told his attorney, "I totally understand your reluctance, so don't worry about it. I'll just get the attorney who set it up for the other company and let them take care of it." Then he added, "By the way, I'm sure the other attorneys won't want to work on just one project, so we'll probably have to give them lots of other work as well."

"Well hold on a minute," his lawyer said. "Let me do some research." Amazingly, his lawyer managed to find a way to make it work. Mitchell got the same resistance from his insurance company and his accountant. In each case, he offered to give the job to the insurance company and accounting firm who set up the daycare center for the other company.[5] They somehow found a way to make it work, and the company opened the daycare center.

At that time, the company had 300 employees. Five years later, that figure almost doubled, and the daycare center had 75 children, 55 of whom had parents or grandparents working there. The effect on employees has been tremendous.

In addition to taking their kids with them to work, other little things the company does make a world of difference to working parents. The company keeps the daycare center staffed until the last parent picks up his or her children, and there is no charge for staying late or working on weekends. Many employees are paid hourly or by the piece they make, so if an employee has to leave work, drive 10 to 20 minutes to his or her child's daycare center to take care of a problem, he or she may lose two hours of work. With the daycare center on-site, Mitchell doesn't even ask employees to clock out if they want to go check on their children. Instead of keeping an eye on the clock every afternoon, getting ready to sprint out to pick up the children, Mitchell Gold's employees can focus on their jobs and they don't have to worry about their children.

Shirley Roberts often works late and wouldn't be able to see her granddaughter very often if it weren't for the company's daycare. "It's wonderful," Shirley said. "I really get to see Cassy a lot more because she's here. We get to eat lunch with them if we want to, we can take them out at break if we want to. She loves it here, and I love her being here."

In addition to her own experience, Shirley believes the daycare center at work has a huge impact on her employees. As a sewing supervisor with 100 people under her charge, she noticed that people who have their children in the company daycare don't miss as much work and they seem to be happier because they know what their children are doing all the time. "I have nothing but good things to say about our daycare."[6]

Even the layout has improved morale. The daycare center is located between the factory and the administrative offices, and it has large windows, so anyone walking by can look in on the children. As you drive up in the parking lot outside, you see the playground. Just having the children nearby gives what Mitchell calls "smiling spirit." "Even when the kids aren't in there, people walk by and smile."

The Mitchell Gold Company doesn't stop at daycare. The company also promotes good health, teaching employees that if they're in good health, they'll be at work more, they'll earn more, and that's good for their family. It also added a gym, and the company cafeteria serves healthy food. Every spring, the company holds a health fair, where every employee gets a free physical. Women get mammograms, and everybody gets checked for glaucoma. Several early cases of breast cancer were detected at health fairs, and, in one case, a very late stage case from someone who had not participated in previous years. She had surgery and treatment, and was back on the road to recovery. She came in later and said, "That saved my life."

While many people argue that their companies can't afford to provide family-friendly services, Mitchell Gold believes they can't afford not to. The results have been dramatic. Although it wasn't his goal, the daycare center and other worker-friendly efforts have paid huge dividends. Of the 75 factories in a 50-mile radius, the Mitchell Gold Company has the highest productivity per employee, the highest profit per employee, and the lowest turnover. "Do these things really cost us money?" Mitchell asked? "I don't think so."

A Steak in the Outcome

Another company that has realized huge profits by putting people first is Outback Steakhouse. When Chris Sullivan and his two partners opened the first Outback Steakhouse in 1988, all three founders were veterans of the restaurant industry. Instead of using the traditional formula, the partners decided to turn managers into owners through a unique profit-sharing formula. The restaurant manager-proprietors sign a five-year contract and put $25,000 of their own money down in return for 10 percent of the cash flow of the restaurant, in addition to a salary and stock options. The deal had the potential to turn $45,000-a-year employees into millionaires, and it worked. About 95 percent of Outback proprietors stay with the company for at least five years—giving the company a huge advantage over its competitors—and about 80 percent renew their five-year contracts.[7]

Because they have a piece of the action, proprietors have a vested interest in running the restaurant right. Not only is turnover lower, but each proprietor pays more attention to hiring and training employees. If customers are unhappy, proprietors feel it in their wallet. By increasing sales, proprietors also increase their own paycheck, and in turn, boost corporate earnings.[8]

Outback Steakhouse took the concept a step further, and gave regional managers 10 percent of the profits in their region, and added a bonus program that gives an astounding 25 percent of the profits of the restaurants back to the employees who work in each restaurant. If the restaurant beats the minimum profit level and increases profit relative to the same quarter a year earlier, every employee who works more than 10 hours a week gets to share in the bonus.

The Outback Steakhouse founders got a lot of "free advice" from industry experts who thought they were giving away the store. After all, why give away up to 45 percent of the profits in each restaurant? The founders' philosophy is simple. Restaurants spend millions each year to recruit and train new managers. If Outback Steakhouse could keep managers longer and get them to act as if they owned the place, they'd have an advantage. This management philosophy puts a premium on trust, ownership, and decentralization, along with a strong belief in sharing the wealth.[9] It also allows the company to be much more decentralized. Because the proprietors are running the show, they need less management supervision—a factor that played a huge role in fueling the company's growth.[10]

Melinda Sowers, the proprietor of Outback in Jacksonville Beach, Florida, started waiting tables in Savannah, Georgia, while she was studying to be an occupational therapist. She had worked in two other restaurants, and when she got the job at Outback, she vowed to never work in another restaurant again. "I've never worked in a restaurant with such a supportive environment," Melinda said. "This is the only restaurant I'd even think about making a career of."[11]

In another departure from conventional wisdom, Outback restaurants are only open for dinner. By focusing entirely on dinner, they can concentrate on doing a great job with one shift. Furthermore, mangers, cooks, and servers have more time to spend with their families or get involved in the community. It also means that employees are fresh, rested, and have a good outlook when they are at work.[12] In addition to earning more than $3 million at each restaurant, the Outback chain consistently sets the standard for high-quality service and customer satisfaction.[13]

Richard "R.J." Luna, proprietor of the Outback in Murfreesboro, Tennessee, spent 10 years working as a bartender and waiting tables before getting the chance to run his own Outback. Like other proprietors, he put up $25,000 of his own money, and he gets 10 percent of the profits. "I love the opportunity," R.J. says. "They made it my college. They've got a great training and development program here, and they've put a lot of trust in me."[14]

R.J. is already grooming the next generation of leaders to follow in his footsteps. Kagee Tate, a bartender and six-year veteran at R.J.'s Outback, was just named a Key Employee, and hopes to open his own Outback Steakhouse someday. "You get a job at any other restaurant, and it's just another restaurant job," Kagee explained. "Here at Outback, it's like playing for the Yankees—it's not just playing baseball."[15]

Take Time to Coach Them

Taking care of your people isn't limited to pay and benefits programs, a huge part of employee care is how you treat your people. Instead of focusing just on profit and efficiency, think about what you can do to create an environment that allows your employees to thrive. Carol Williams learned early in her career how important it was to have a supportive boss.

As a brand new copywriter at Leo Burnett, a renowned ad agency in Chicago, Carol approached the creative director with an idea for Pillsbury, the firm's largest client. The agency was working on a campaign to promote biscuits in the morning, and Carol's idea for the tagline "It's Pillsbury's Best Time of Day" became a central theme of the campaign. She went on to launch the "Say Hello to Pop-in-Fresh Dough" campaign for Pillsbury, which reintroduced the Dough Boy into American homes and advertising history.[16]

As a young African-American woman in the late 1960s, the deck was decidedly stacked against Carol, but she demonstrated a creative flair and willingness to work hard. She wasn't afraid to step up with a new idea or to take on challenging assignments. Over the years, several industry veterans took time to coach and mentor her, which gave her the skills and the confidence to continue rising through the ranks.

"I got to watch those great minds work, see their leadership, how they embrace creativity and smart thinking," Carol said. "They were very nurturing, even though this was in the late 60s and early 70s, those men embraced me and guided me. I'm not saying that whole concept was widespread, but that is the way they approached me, and as a result, I blossomed."

When her boss gave her the Secret account, first he made her promise not to quit. At the time, Secret was the number-nine antiperspirant brand, and was widely known as the choice of little old ladies with blue hair. Despite that reputation, the product itself was very strong and incredibly effective. Carol knew from her personal experience that the women in Secret's target market worked very hard all day, but they still wanted to look good at the end of the day. Carol captured this idea in one sentence: "Strong enough for a man, but made for a woman." This simple truth told the story and struck a chord. Within six months, Secret was the number-one selling brand in the country, and it held that position for the next 25 years.

When Carol started her own agency, she lived by the same principles that helped her in her own career. Instead of just focusing on getting the job done, she works hard to coach and develop her employees as people—both at work and in their private lives. "My job is developing, guiding, and nurturing talent, and creating the framework within which they can thrive," Carol said. "I try to approach the young people who come under my tutelage in the same manner. To go a little bit beyond their creativity. Are you willing to support them in their personal aspects? Their challenges in life itself?"[17]

Bright young minds from all over the country flock to Oakland, California, for a chance to work with Carol, the advertising prodigy turned teacher. By focusing on developing her people and nurturing their talent, she grew Carol H. Williams Advertising into the largest African-American–owned ad agency in the United States, with $130 million in annual revenues and clients such as General Motors, Allstate Insurance, BP Amoco, and Frito-Lay.

People Are Your Best Investment

Taking care of your people isn't limited to your employees. It also means taking care of other people on whom your company depends. At Brighton Collectibles, Jerry Kohl goes to great lengths to help store owners operate more efficiently and succeed in business. In addition to helping them manage their inventory more efficiently, Brighton regularly takes groups of store owners overseas on trips that are part reward and part education.

He brought a group of 80 shop owners to China to visit a factory that was making watches for them. The next year, Brighton took 110 store owners on a 10-day, all-expense-paid trip to Maui. There was nothing for sale, no order forms, and no chance to buy anything. Instead, Jerry hired speakers to teach classes on various topics such as hiring, marketing, and accounting to help the shop owners stay in business. More than anything else, the shop owners are an investment in the future. Jerry realizes these independent shop owners are key ingredients in his success.

"In a department store they teach you how to put things on sale," Jerry said. "We teach them how to bring people into the store." The other benefit is that shop owners have time to talk with one another, compare notes, and share ideas. "When you put together 100 people who are all entrepreneurs, and give them enough time to sit and talk, they walk away with hundreds of ideas."[18]

As one customer pointed out, these were people for whom most companies wouldn't even buy a diet soda when they go to New York for a trade show, and Brighton put them up in a five star resort. By rewarding them, helping them and working closely with them to make them successful, they both benefit.

Bob Stiller does the same thing at Green Mountain Coffee Roasters, putting corporate philanthropy to work in the company's own supply chain. Green Mountain lets employees take paid time off to work on projects of their choice, and gives 5 percent of pretax profits to charitable organizations. Instead of just writing a check, Green Mountain focuses on improving the quality of life for coffee farmers in their own supply chain, which truly makes it a virtuous circle.

More than 20 percent of Green Mountain's 600 employees have spent time on coffee farms in South America and Indonesia working on projects such as building new drying patios to help farmers improve the quality of their coffee, planting vegetable gardens to help feed the villages, and generally helping improve the quality of life. Green Mountain even brought 60 coffee farmers from developing countries to Boston for a conference on best practices—teaching them ways to be more efficient and improve their coffee crop.

It's All About People

A key reason companies such as 99 Cents Only, Green Mountain Coffee Roasters, Brighton Collectibles, and Outback Steakhouse have done so well over the long haul is the way they treat their people. Sure, they have to have a good product and a compelling offer for the customer, or they wouldn't even get out of the starting gate. Each company's real competitive advantage is the human element underlying everything they do.

It takes more than pay and perks to create a winning climate, although they are certainly factors. Just as important, though, is the human factor. Do your people enjoy being at work? Do they feel important and valued? Taking time to coach and develop your employees is just as critical to your company's future success.

"Make sure you take care of your people," says JetBlue CEO David Neeleman. "We live in a service environment. I think there is a temptation to be so cheap with your people because you want to be successful. You just have to really take care of those people."

Conclusion

There is no magic formula for success in business, and no silver bullet that will work in every situation. Every company is different, and the challenges you face are constantly changing. If you can learn from others who have gone before you, though, you can avoid making the same mistakes and find new ideas that help in your business. As you read about successful leaders, some familiar themes emerge. Listen to your customers. Take care of your people. Lead by example. It's advice that's easy to give, but it's amazing how many companies don't follow it. At times you can get so caught up in the rules and procedures that you don't consider what they mean to your employees or customers.

As Roger Berkowitz discovered at Legal Seafoods, asking your employees for advice can help solve the trickiest problems. Carlos Ghosn rescued Nissan by getting employees involved in the decision-making process, turning the culture around and revitalizing the company. Rich Teerlink did the same thing at Harley-Davidson, demonstrating that American manufacturers not only can survive but prosper in a competitive global economy. Harley racked up an unprecedented series of sales and profits by putting decision-making authority in the hands of the people doing the work on the front lines. It's a simple concept, but far too few companies actually encourage employees to take charge and make decisions.

Sometimes the best strategy is to take the path less traveled. Victor and Janie Tsao went out of their way to avoid competing with Cisco, knowing they could never take on the networking powerhouse in the business market. Instead, they focused Linksys on home networking—a market that barely existed at the time. In the process, Linksys became attractive to Cisco precisely because it was in a different market, and Cisco later bought the company for $500 million. Trader Joe's, Outback Steakhouse, and easyJet all avoided the competition, successfully carving out a niche in their respective industries by going around the competition.

Taking the path less traveled can yield big rewards in other areas as well. David Neeleman eliminated costly call centers and improved morale at JetBlue by having every reservation agent in the company work from home. With no commute or rush-hour traffic and flexible schedules, is it any surprise that the JetBlue reservations agents always seem to be in a good mood?

Sometimes winning strategies are surprisingly simple. Although it sounds counterintuitive, undermining your business today can ensure your long-term success. Ron Shaich took a bold gamble, selling Au Bon Pain so he could focus on building Panera Bread. Clodhoppers, Blockbuster Video, and PayPal all found themselves in a similar position, and all found success by ditching their earlier strategies and moving in a new direction.

Leveraging the idea lets you spend your time and resources in your strongest areas, while taking advantage of your partners' strengths in other areas. Jim Koch took the unprecedented step of outsourcing his brewing operations, letting him actually *increase* the quality of Samuel Adams beer. Bill Sweedler saved JOE BOXER by making a groundbreaking deal with Kmart, drastically increasing sales while cutting the complexity of the company's operations. In one bold step, he rebuilt JOE BOXER into a leading brand with a solid foundation. Instead of trying to do everything themselves, these visionary leaders focused on their leverage points and opened the door to much larger opportunities.

One underlying theme great leaders consistently demonstrate is taking care of their people. Marilyn Carlson Nelson at Carlson Companies, Dave Gold at 99 Cents Only, and Chris Sullivan at Outback Steakhouse all invested extra time and money in their employees. In the process, they realized significant growth and profits and built their companies into industry leaders. Jerry Kohl at Brighton Collectibles and Bob Stiller at Green Mountain Coffee took it one step further, investing in their outside partners to ensure their companies' success. Don't underestimate the human factor in everything you do—people are the best investment you can make.

Bernie Marcus and Arthur Blank built Home Depot into a $30-billion business by relentlessly focusing on their customers and their employees. After the founders retired, the company ran into problems when cost-cutting measures aimed at increasing profits undercut its core culture, alienating both customers and employees. The exact opposite happened at Costco. Jim Sinegal had the courage to risk the ire of Wall Street, putting his employees and customers ahead of quarterly profits. That may not help the company's stock in the short term, but it's the way to build an enduring business over the long haul.

In the ever-changing landscape of business, there is no blueprint for success. The rules are constantly changing in the middle of the game. As these leaders have demonstrated, you can succeed against long odds and tough competitors if you're willing to think creatively, stay flexible, and learn from your mistakes—or the mistakes of others before you. In the process, you can help rewrite the rules in your industry and build a lasting business.

Chapter Notes

Chapter 1

[1] David Neeleman, interview with the author, January 5, 2003.

[2] Sydney Finkelstein, *Why Smart Executives Fail* (New York: Portfolio, 2003), 118.

[3] Bernie Marcus, Arthur Blank, and Bob Andelman, *Built From Scratch: How a Couple of Regular Guys Grew The Home Depot from Nothing to $30 Billion* (New York: Random House, 1999), 259.

[4] Chris Roush, *Inside Home Depot* (New York: McGraw-Hill, 1999), 45.

[5] Marcus and Blank, *Built From Scratch*, 260.

[6] "Arthur Blank just another rookie at camp," *NFL.com* wire reports, July 25, 2002.

[7] Arthur Blank, "First Person," *NFL Insider*, Postseason issue, 2002.

[8] Marilyn Carlson Nelson, Keynote speech to the 16th Annual Multicultural Forum, Minneapolis Minnesota, February 5, 2004.

[9] Marilyn Carlson Nelson, interview with the author, March 15, 2004.

[10] Ibid.

[11] Marilyn Carlson Nelson, Keynote speech to the 16th Annual Multicultural Forum.

[12] Carol Williams, interview with the author, February 9, 2004.

Chapter 2

[1] Dan Firestone, interview with the author, September 13, 2001.

[2] John Shields, interview with the author, January 6, 2004.

[3] Ibid.

[4] Amy Wu, "Affordable quality sells Trader Joe's," *The New York Times*, August 10, 2003.

[5] Shields interview.

[6] Wu, "Affordable quality sells Trader Joe's."

7 Larry Armstrong, "Trader Joe's Atlantic Overtures," *BusinessWeek*, June 5, 1995.

8 Ian Mount, "Be Fast, Be Frugal, Be Right," *Inc.*, January 2004.

9 Jon Fortt, "Linksys' hustle pays off big," *Mercury News*, April 14, 2003.

10 Mount, "Be Fast, Be Frugal, Be Right."

11 Victor Tsao, interview with the author, January 14, 2004.

12 Fortt, "Linksys' hustle pays off big."

13 Michael Garry, "In P&G Marriage, Iams Takes IT Slow," *Consumer Goods*, February 2002.

14 Arlene Weintraub, "PETsMART Tries for a New Leash on Life," *BusinessWeek*, January 24, 2001.

15 Amy Tsao, "Two Stocks in the Pet Penthouse," *BusinessWeek*, October 2, 2003.

16 Weintraub, "PETsMART Tries for a New Leash on Life."

17 Christine Mumford, interview with the author, December 21, 2003.

18 Robert Barker, "The Money in Creature Comforts," *BusinessWeek*, September 23, 2002.

19 PETCO 2002 Annual Report.

20 PETsMART 2002 Annual Report.

21 Joanna Walters, "Making it all look easy," *The Observer*, April 21, 2002.

22 "Airline Settlement Agreement Reached," Long Beach City Council, February 28, 2003.

Chapter 3

1 Julie Rose, "How We Began: From burgers to beer to Berthas, nine innovators tell their tales of grit, luck, and inspiration," *Fortune Small Business*, April 17, 2000.

2 Jim Koch, interview with the author, December 17, 2003.

3 Jim Koch, interview with the author, December 19, 2003.

4 Robert Mamis, "Market Maker," *Inc.*, December 1995.

5 Koch interview, December 17, 2003.

6 "His Doughnut Stores Are His Children," *BusinessWeek*, December 9, 2002.

7 Kirk Kazanjian and Amy Joyner, *Making Dough: The 12 Secrets of Krispy Kreme's Sweet Success* (Hoboken, N.J.: John Wiley & Sons, 2004), 35.

8 Scott Hume, "Model Behavior: Krispy Kreme's Livengood Happily Handles Dozens of Hot Opportunities," *Restaurants and Institutions*, July 1, 2001.

9 Krispy Kreme 2003 Annual Report.

10 Penelope Patsuris, "Krispy Kreme Takes a Bite Out of Britain," *Forbes*, November 14, 2002.

11 Colette Landi Sipperly, interview with the author, January 23, 2004.

12 JOE BOXER corporate history, retrieved from *www.joeboxer.com*.

13 Bill Sweedler, interview with the author, January 20, 2004.

14 "Kmart, JOE BOXER sign deal," *DSN Retailing Today*, September 17, 2001.

15 Mike Duff, "Kmart launches JOE BOXER line: new apparel, home goods line designed to lure younger consumers," *DSN Retailing Today*, August 12, 2002.

16 Sweedler interview.

17 Duff, "Kmart launches JOE BOXER line: new apparel, home goods line designed to lure younger consumers."

Chapter 4

1 Gretchen Morgenson, *Forbes Great Minds of Business* (New York: John Wiley & Sons, 1997), 45.

2 Gary Hoover, interview with the author, November 3, 2003.

3 Gordon Bethune, *From Worst to First* (New York: John Wiley & Sons, 1999), 102.

4 Ibid., 105.

5 Gordon Bethune, interview on *News Hour with Jim Lehrer*, March 19, 1998.

6 Dawn Gilbertson, "Problem-solver key to America West's recovery," *The Arizona Republic*, January 11, 2004.

7 John H. Johnson, *Succeeding Against the Odds* (New York: Warner Books, 1989), 134–35.

8 "Krispy Kreme CEO Scott Livengood Discusses the Allure of Hot Doughnuts," *BizEd*, May/June 2003.

9 David Farkas, "Dealing With Paradox," *Chain Leader*, October 2001.

10 Lawrence Perlman, interview with the author, January 23, 2004.

11 Laura Liebeck, "Mixing Discipline with Disney," *Discount Store News*, September 17, 1990.

12 Laura Rowley, *On Target: How the World's Hottest Retailer Hit a Bull's-Eye* (Hoboken, N.J.: John Wiley & Sons, 2003), 67–68.

13 "General Mills Generalizes," *The Associated Press*, April 7, 2003.

14 Ibid.

Chapter 5

1 In-N-Out corporate history, retrieved from *www.in-n-out.com*.

2 Greg Hernandez, "Traditional In-N-Out Burger Faces an Uncertain Future," *The Los Angeles Times*, July 2, 2000.

3 Greg Johnson, "More Than Fare; A Simple Menu, Customer Service and a Familial Touch Prove to Be a Recipe That's Working for In-N-Out," *The Los Angeles Times*, August 15, 1997.

4 Deborah Silver, "Primary Choices," *Restaurants & Institutions*, March 2000.

5 "The Popular Vote," *Restaurants & Institutions*, March 2003.

6 Hernandez, "Traditional In-N-Out Burger Faces an Uncertain Future."

7 Aldo Svaldi, "Market cap pushes Yahoo past Baby Bell," *Denver Business Journal*, January 25, 1999.

8 Larry Page, interview with the author, October 17, 2003.

9 Ibid.

10 Eileen Gunn, "Was John Doerr Right?," *Internet World*, July 15, 1999.

11 Page interview.

[12] Dale Fuller, interview with the author, January 22, 2002.

[13] Linda Tischler, "Borland Software: Back in the Black," *Fast Company*, July 2002.

[14] Kevin Maney, "A feel-good tech story: Borland hit bottom, bounced back," *USA Today*, October 22, 2002.

[15] Fuller interview.

[16] Maney, "A feel-good tech story: Borland hit bottom, bounced back."

[17] Clare Haney, "Inprise/Borland embraces Apple," *InfoWorld*, July 11, 2000.

[18] Martin LaMonica, "Borland has designs on .Net developers," *ZDNet*, February 5, 2003.

[19] Haney, "Inprise/Borland embraces Apple."

Chapter 6

[1] Peter Thiel, interview with the author, December 1, 2003.

[2] Deirdre McMurdy, "Building future on sweet idea," *Financial Post*, February 11, 2002.

[3] Chris Emery and Larry Finnson, interview with the author, October 9, 2003.

[4] Julie Sloan, "Grandmothered Into Business," *Fortune Small Business*, February 4, 2003.

[5] Carol Hymowitz, "Panera CEO's Recipe: Learn From the Past, Anticipate Trends," *The Wall Street Journal*, June 10, 2003.

[6] Ibid.

[7] Michael Silverstein and Neil Fiske, *Trading Up* (Boston: The Boston Consulting Group, 2003), 115.

[8] Interview with Ronald Schaich, *Neil Cavuto on Your World*, Fox News, November 14, 2002.

[9] Ibid.

[10] Panera Bread Q4 Earnings Report, February 19, 2004.

[11] "Panera Bread: An Appetizing Stock," *BusinessWeek*, March 25, 2002.

[12] Gerard P. Cachon and Martin A. Lariviere, "Supply Chain Coordination with Revenue-Sharing Contracts: Strength and Limitations" (research paper).

[13] E. Shapiro, "Blockbuster Seeks a New Deal with Hollywood," *The Wall Street Journal*, March 25, 1998.

[14] Sumner Redstone, *A Passion to Win* (New York: Simon & Schuster, 2001), 284–5.

[15] Sumner Redstone, speech to The Commonwealth Club, June 15, 2001.

[16] Robert Lenzner, "The Vindication of Sumner Redstone," *Forbes*, June 15, 1998.

[17] E. Shapiro, "Blockbuster's return is on fast forward, says CEO with Big Plans for Rentals," *The Wall Street Journal*, April 7, 1998.

[18] Several small video chains later sued Blockbuster and the studios, alleging that revenue sharing was anti-competitive. The judge threw the case out when one of the video store owners admitted that he had never asked the studios for a similar revenue sharing agreement.

Chapter 7

[1] Gert Boyle, interview with the author, January 28, 2003.

[2] Andrew Kramer, "Columbia Sportswear gains on retail rivals," *The Daily Camera*, January 6, 2003.

[3] "Gert Gets the Last Laugh," *BusinessWeek*, June 10, 2002.

[4] Vicky Uhland, "Why Jacket Sales Continue to Climb," *Wearables Business*, August 1, 1999.

[5] John D. Thomas, "Big Bertha and Me," *Emory Magazine*, Winter 1997.

[6] Callaway Golf company history, retrieved from *www.callawaygolf.com*.

[7] Doug Ferguson, "Golf Equipment Pioneer Dies of Cancer," *USA Today*, July 6, 2001.

[8] Richard Tait, interview with the author, December 2001.

[9] John Osher, interview with the author, March 19, 2003.

[10] "Why P&G's Smile Is So Bright," *BusinessWeek*, August 1, 2002.

Chapter 8

[1] Chris Emery and Larry Finnson, interview with the author, October 9, 2003.

[2] Julie Sloan, "Grandmothered Into Business," *Fortune Small Business*, February 4, 2003.

[3] Joanna Walters, "Making it all look easy," *The Observer*, April 21, 2002.

[4] Charles Goldsmith, "British Airways Launches No-Frills Unit; Critics Fret," *The Wall Street Journal*, May 22, 1998.

[5] Ibid.

[6] Richard Morais, "From tragedy, a fortune," *Forbes*, July 9, 2001.

[7] Scott Kirsner, "Stelios Makes Growth Look Easy," *Fast Company*, November 2002, 64.

[8] Pat Regnier, "Easy Goes It," *Time Europe*, May 20, 2002.

[9] Fred "Chico" Lager, *Ben & Jerry's: The Inside Scoop* (New York: Crown Publishers, 1994), 112–117.

[10] Ibid., 120.

[11] "The Value of Free Publicity," *Fast Company*, November 2002.

[12] Dave Gold, interview with the author, October 31, 2003.

[13] Richard Tait, interview with the author, November 27, 2001.

[14] Julie Bick, "Inside the Smartest Little Company in America," *Inc.*, January 1, 2002.

[15] John H. Johnson, *Succeeding Against the Odds* (New York: Warner Books), 125–27.

[16] Ibid., 128.

[17] Donna Shew, "Barney Creator Sheryl Leach: She Relied on Common Sense to Help Her Build a Purple Empire," *Investor's Business Daily*, July 29, 1999.

[18] Tom Richman, "Selling to Your Customer's Customer," *Inc.*, August 1991.

[19] "Barney History," Character Products.com.

[20] Stephanie Anderson, "Wouldn't You Like to Knock the Stuffing Out of Barney?" *BusinessWeek*, August 16, 1993.

[21] HIT Entertainment, *2001 Annual Report*.

[22] Kerry Capell, "The House that Bob Built," *BusinessWeek*, April 8, 2002.

[23] James Koch, "Portrait of the CEO as Salesman," *Inc.*, March 1988.

[24] Jim Koch, interview with the author, December 17, 2003.

[25] Ibid.

[26] Robert Mamis, "Market Marker," *Inc.*, December 1995.

[27] Gerry Khermouch, "Keeping the Froth on Sam Adams," *BusinessWeek*, August 21, 2003.

[28] James Koch, "Portrait of the CEO as Salesman," *Inc.*, March 1988

[29] Bob Brooke, "Emma Chappell founded a bank of her own," *Philadelphia Business Journal*, December 7, 1988.

[30] Ibid.

[31] Derek Dingle, "Lessons from the Top: Advice from three of the top black-owned businesses," *Black Enterprise*, May 1999.

[32] Jeremy Quittner, "A Black Entrepreneur in Banking Gives Others a Break," *BusinessWeek*, June 30, 1999.

[33] Jeremy Quittner, "A Community Bank Founder's Secret: Never Take No For an Answer," *BusinessWeek*, July 6, 1999.

Chapter 9

[1] John McAdam, interview with the author, December 17, 2001.

[2] Norm Brodsky, "Street Smarts: The Path to the Top," *Inc.*, February 2003.

[3] Norm Brodsky, "A Niche in Time," *Inc.*, February 1997.

[4] "Starbucks Dumps USA Today, Inks with New York Times," *Brandweek*, August 7, 2000.

[5] Anthony Ramirez, "Times Talk: Starbucks," *The New York Times*, March 2002.

[6] Scott Cook, "Software by the Numbers," *Fortune Small Business*, March 8, 1999.

[7] Suzanne Taylor and Kathy Schroeder, *Inside Intuit* (Boston: Harvard Business School Press, 2003), 9.

[8] Geoffrey A. Moore, *Crossing the Chasm* (New York: Harper Business, 1991), 146.

[9] Cook, "Software by the Numbers."

[10] "Using Customers as Beta Testers," *Inc.*, January 1995.

[11] Ibid.

[12] Taylor and Schroeder, *Inside Intuit*, 72.

[13] Eric Nee, "The Hottest CEO in Tech," *Business 2.0*, June 2003.

[14] Taylor and Schroeder, pp. 74-75.

[15] Ibid., 72.

[16] Troy Wolverton, "Billpoint Failure a Lesson for eBay?," *CNET*, July 8, 2002.

[17] Bill Menezes and Monica Alleven, "Handsets: Promises, Promises," *Wireless Week*, May 18, 1998.

[18] "Motorola's Galvin Shakes Things Up—Again," *BusinessWeek*, May 28, 2001.
[19] Bruce Felps, "Motorola Making Up Digital Ground," *Wireless Week*, May 31, 1999.
[20] Michael Kenellos, "Intel Gears Up for Prescott, Wireless," *CNET*, May 15, 2003.
[21] Don Clark, "Big Bet Behind Intel Comeback: In Chips, Speed Isn't Everything," *The Wall Street Journal*, November 18, 2003.
[22] David Kirkpatrick, "At Intel, Speed Isn't Everything," *Fortune*, February 9, 2004.
[23] John Spooner, "Intel Tweaks Roadmap to Boost Pentium M," *CNET*, May 29, 2003.
[24] Therese Poletti, "Intel's earnings beat estimates," *Mercury News*, July 15, 2003.
[25] Phil Schlein, interview with the author, November 28, 2001.

Chapter 10

[1] Wayne Inouye, interview with the author, November 25, 2003.
[2] Arik Hesseldahl, "The McDonald's of Computers," *Forbes*, November 24, 2003.
[3] Dave Duffield, interview with the author, November 30, 2001.
[4] Victor Tsao, interview with the author, January 14, 2004.
[5] Chris Roush, *Inside Home Depot* (New York: McGraw-Hill, 1999), 89.
[6] Marcus, Blank, and Andelman, *Built From Scratch*, 142.
[7] Ibid., 143.
[8] "Separating Home Depot from the Pack," *National Home Center News*, December 27, 1999.
[9] Roush, Inside Home Depot, 90–91.
[10] Marcus, Blank, and Andelman, *Built From Scratch*, 273.

Chapter 11

[1] David Adams, "Cincinnati Bell rings the bell," *The Akron Beacon Journal*, June 22, 1997.
[2] John LaMacchia, interview with the author, December 10, 2001.
[3] Jim McCann, *Stop and Sell the Roses* (New York: Random House, 1998), 100–101.
[4] Jim McCann, interview with the author, December 13, 2001.
[5] McCann, *Stop and Sell the Roses*, 102.
[6] Cindy McCaffrey, interview with the author, September 9, 2003.
[7] Scott S. Smith, "Betting On Success," *Entrepreneur*, August 1999.
[8] "The Bob Johnson Factor: How the BET Founder Is Building an Empire," *Knowledge at Wharton*, January 14, 2004.
[9] Robert Johnson, "The Market Nobody Wanted," *Fortune Small Business*, August 1, 2002.
[10] "The Bob Johnson Factor: How the BET Founder Is Building an Empire."
[11] Johnson, "The Market Nobody Wanted."

[12] Jeremy Brosowsky, "The Color of Success," *Washington Business Forward*, October 1999.

[13] "Viacom completes BET deal," *Washington Business Journal*, January 23, 2001.

[14] Smith, "Betting On Success."

[15] Brent Schlender, "Steve Jobs' Amazing Movie Adventure," *Fortune*, September 18, 1995.

[16] Pixar company history, retrieved from *www.pixar.com*.

[17] Justin Martin, "Inside the Pixar Dream Factory," *Fortune Small Business*, February 1, 2003.

[18] Jeanette White, interview with the author, February 23, 2004.

[19] Ellen McCarthy, "A Master of Change and Challenge," *The Washington Post*, December 25, 2001.

Chapter 12

[1] Bill George, "Wanted: Authentic Leaders," *The Wall Street Journal*, December 15, 2003.

[2] Rich Teerlink, interview with the author, February 4, 2004

[3] Marcus, Blank, and Andelman, *Built From Scratch*, 269.

[4] Curt Schleier, "Home Depot's Arthur Blank and Bernie Marcus: They Rose to the Top by Putting Customers First," *Investor's Business Daily*, July 8, 1999.

[5] Robert Nardelli, "Lessons from the CEO Academy," in *How to Run a Company: Lessons from Top Leaders of the CEO Academy* (New York: Crown Business, 2003).

[6] Steve Matthews, "Home Depot Improvement Project: CEO Rebuilds Sales, Service," *The Seattle Times*, August 19, 2003.

[7] Aixa Pascual, "Tidying Up at Home Depot," *BusinessWeek*, November 26, 2001.

[8] Peter Cohan, "Jack Welch and Cost of Corporate Legends," *Gurus Online*, December 30, 2002.

[9] Dean Foust, "What Worked at GE Isn't Working at Home Depot," *BusinessWeek*, January 27, 2003.

[10] "Faces in the News," *Forbes*, May 29, 2002.

[11] "Blank: Home Depot Should Focus on Customers," *Atlanta Business Chronicle*, February 26, 2003.

[12] John Helyar, "The Only Company Wal-Mart Fears," *Fortune*, November 24, 2003.

[13] Jim Sinegal, speech to the Portland State University's Food Industry Leadership Center, October 21, 2003.

[14] Robin Goldwyn Blumenthal, "Pricey Club," *Barron's*, May 17, 1999.

[15] Ann Zimmerman, "Costco Slashes Profit Outlook for Fourth Quarter and 2003," *The Wall Street Journal*, August 6, 2003.

[16] Nanette Byrnes, et al., "The Good CEO," *BusinessWeek*, September 23, 2002.

[17] "James Sinegal, Costco: The Bargain Hunter," *BusinessWeek*, September 23, 2002.

[18] Helyar, "The Only Company Wal-Mart Fears."

[19] Ibid.

[20] Kregg Jodie, interview with the author, December 22, 2003.

[21] Ibid.

[22] Jim Underwood, *More Than a Pink Cadillac* (New York: McGraw-Hill, 2002), 64.

[23] George, "Wanted: Authentic Leaders."

[24] Jeffrey Pfeffer, "More Mr. Nice Guy," *Business 2.0*, December 2003.

Chapter 13

[1] Roger Berkowitz, interview with the author, December 17, 2003.

[2] Alex Taylor III, "The Man Who Vows To Change Japan Inc.," *Fortune*, December 20, 1999.

[3] Emily Thornton, "Remaking Nissan," *BusinessWeek*, November 15, 1999.

[4] Joseph White, "From the Brink of Disaster," *The Wall Street Journal*, January 31, 2003.

[5] David Magee, *Turnaround: How Carlos Ghosn Rescued Nissan* (New York: Harper Business, 2003), 66.

[6] Alex Taylor III, "Nissan's Turnaround Artist: Carlos Ghosn Is Giving Japan a Lesson in How to Compete," *Fortune*, February 7, 2002.

[7] Magee, Turnaround: How Carlos Ghosn Rescued Nissan, 67–71.

[8] Joseph White, "From the Brink of Disaster," *The Wall Street Journal*, January 31, 2003.

[9] Reiji Yoshida, "Foreign managers bring change to corporate life," *The Japan Times*, May 24, 2001.

[10] White, "From the Brink of Disaster."

[11] Yoshio Takahashi, "Nissan Continues its Profitable Drive," *Dow Jones Newswires*, August 26, 2003.

[12] Rich Teerlink and Lee Ozley, *More Than a Motorcycle* (Boston: Harvard Business School Press, 2000), 8–10.

[13] Rich Teerlink, interview with the author, February 4, 2004.

[14] Ibid.

[15] Teerlink and Ozley, *More Than a Motorcycle*, 99–105.

[16] Teerlink interview.

[17] Gina Imperato, "Harley Shifts Gears," *Fast Company*, June/July 1997.

[18] Teerlink and Ozley, *More Than a Motorcycle*, 140.

[19] Jeffrey Bleustein, Speech to the Summit on the 21st Century Workforce, June 20, 2001.

[20] Ibid.

[21] Joe Cooper, interview with the author, January 14, 2004.

[22] Teerlink interview.

[23] Theodore Kinni, "The Art of the Appreciative Inquiry," *Working Knowledge*, September 22, 2003.

[24] Bob Stiller, interview with the author, February 9, 2004.

[25] Joanne Gordon, "Meet the Freight Fairy," *Forbes*, January 20, 2003.

[26] Kinni, "The Art of the Appreciative Inquiry."

[27] Gordon, "Meet the Freight Fairy."

Chapter 14

[1] Lou Pritchett, interview with the author, February 1, 2004.

[2] Lou Pritchett, *Stop Paddling and Start Rocking the Boat* (India: East West Publishing (Madras), 1999), 124–25.

[3] Ibid., 127.

[4] Pritchett interview.

[5] Arlene Weintraub, "Powering Up at eMachines," *BusinessWeek*, November 17, 2003.

[6] Wayne Inouye, interview with the author, November 25, 2003.

[7] Ibid.

[8] Weintraub, "Powering Up at eMachines."

[9] Arik Hesseldahl, "The McDonald's of Computers," *Forbes*, November 24, 2003.

[10] John Case, "A Business Transformed," *Inc.,* June 1993.

[11] Jerry Kohl, interview with the author, February 10, 2004.

[12] Kevin Kelleher, "66,207,896 Bottles of Beer on the Wall," *Business 2.0*, February 2004.

[13] Ibid.

[14] Anheuser-Busch Investor Presentation, November 2003, retrieved from *www.anheuser-busch.com*.

[15] Ray Rodriguez, interview with the author, February 10, 2004.

Chapter 15

[1] Missy Sullivan, "High-Octane Hog," *Forbes*, September 10, 2001.

[2] Pritchett, *Stop Paddling and Start Rocking the Boat*, 25.

[3] Pritchett interview.

[4] Ibid.

[5] "The Philosophy of Vendor Partnership," *Discount Store News*, October 1999.

[6] Pritchett, *Stop Paddling and Start Rocking the Boat*, 33.

[7] Taylor and Schroeder, *Inside Intuit*, 77–78.

[8] Ibid., 100–101.

[9] Louis Corrigan, "Intuit-ing the Internet," *The Motley Fool*, February 25, 1998.

[10] Allison Green, Intuit, e-mail to the author, December 1, 2003.

[11] "A Sandwich Empire," *American Way*, December 15, 2003.

[12] Ron Joyce, interview with the author, January 23, 2004.

[13] Brent Schlender, "Steve Jobs' Amazing Movie Adventure," *Fortune*, September 18, 1995.

[14] David Shook, "Can Pixar Keep Drawing Investors?" *BusinessWeek*, August 19, 2002.

[15] Richard Verrier and Claudia Eller, "Disney-Pixar split was personal, insiders say," *Los Angeles Times*, February 3, 2004.

[16] Dan Ackman, "Pixar's Business Sequel," *Forbes*, January 30, 2004.

[17] Michael McCarthy, "Dream ends for Disney, Pixar," *USA Today*, January 29, 2004.

[18] Bruce Orwall, "Can Disney Still Rule Animation After Pixar?" *The Wall Street Journal*, February 2, 2004.

[19] Robert A. Lutz, *GUTS! 8 Laws of Business from One of the Most Innovative Business Leaders of Our Time* (New York: John Wiley & Sons, 1999), 38.

[20] Pritchett, *Stop Paddling and Start Rocking the Boat*, 52.

Chapter 16

[1] Bill George, interview with the author, February 18, 2002.

[2] David Whitford, "Medtronic: A Human Place to Work," *Fortune*, January 8, 2001.

[3] "Building A Mission-Driven, Values-Centered Organization." Speech by William W. George, Chairman and CEO, Medtronic, delivered to the Premier CEOs, Aspen, Colorado, September 17, 1998.

[4] William W. George speech.

[5] eWeek.

[6] Sheldon Laube, interview with the author, December 13, 2001.

[7] Tait interview, December 2001.

[8] John Peterman, "The Rise and Fall of the J. Peterman Company," *Harvard Business Review*, September-October, 1999, 62.

[9] Ibid.

[10] Ibid., 61.

[11] Howard Shultz, *Pour Your Heart Into It* (Westport, Conn.: Hyperion Press, 1999), 52.

[12] Ibid.

[13] Jeffrey Garten, *The Mind of the CEO* (New York: Basic Books, 2001), 113.

[14] Marc Allen, *Visionary Business* (Novato, Calif.: New World Library, 1995).

Chapter 17

[1] Brendan Coffey, "The Forbes 400: Every Penny Counts," *Forbes*, September 30, 2002.

[2] Jill Birnbaum, interview with the author, October 31, 2003.

[3] James Ricci, "Taking $5 wine seriously," *Los Angeles Times*, January 8, 2003.

[4] Dave Gold, interview with the author, October 31, 2003.

[5] Bettijane Levine, "Buy low, live high: How a maverick mogul knew the price was right," *The Los Angeles Times,* Jan 4, 2003.

[6] Roger Berkowitz, interview with the author, December 17, 2003.

[7] Justin Martin, "Inside the Pixar Dream Factory," *Fortune Small Business*, February 1, 2003.

[8] Jim Koch, interview with the author, December 17, 2003.

[9] Robert Mamis, "Market Maker," *Inc.*, December 1995.

[10] Koch interview.

Chapter 18

[1] De 'Ann Weimer, "Carlson's Marilyn Nelson: 'I Want to Lead With Love, Not Fear,'" *BusinessWeek*, August 15, 1998.

[2] Marilyn Carlson Nelson, interview with the author, March 15, 2004.

[3] Trudy Rautio, e-mail to the author, February 24, 2004.

[4] Chris Roush, *Inside Home Depot* (New York: McGraw-Hill, 1999), 45.

[5] Mitchell Gold, interview with the author, February 18, 2004.

[6] Shirley Roberts, interview with the author, March 12, 2004.

[7] Verne Harnish, "The X Factor," *Fortune Small Business*, December 1, 2002.

[8] Travis Doster, "Outback Steakhouse Builds Success One Manager at a Time," *NWA Online*, September 26, 1999.

[9] Chris Sullivan, interview with *Michigan Restaurant*.

[10] Jay Finegan, "Unconventional Wisdom," *Inc.*, December 1994.

[11] Melinda Sowers, interview with the author, December 22, 2003.

[12] Charles Bernstein, "Outback to the Future," *Chain Leader*, October 1999.

[13] Charles Bernstein, "At Steak: Newcomers Chase the Leader, Outback," *Restaurants & Institutions*, March 15, 1997.

[14] Richard "R.J." Luna, interview with the author, December 20, 2003.

[15] Kagee Tate, interview with the author, December 20, 2003.

[16] Cassandra Hayes, "Not Just An Ol'Boys Club," *Black Enterprise*, June 1999.

[17] Carol Williams, interview with the author, February 19, 2004.

[18] Jerry Kohl, interview with the author, February 10, 2004.

Index

About the Author

MIKE MERRILL has been a CEO for more than 15 years. As the founder and CEO of Totally Wireless, he was an early pioneer of wireless data, opening the nation's first retail chain dedicated exclusively to wireless products and services. As CEO of ePhones, he raised $28 million in venture capital funding, and provided wireless Internet technology, infrastructure, logistics, and support for more than 300 companies nationwide, including Charles Schwab & Co., Costco, and Aether Systems. He is currently CEO of Smartphones Technologies, and he is an investor in or advisor to several start-up companies.

He is a graduate of the U.S. Military Academy at West Point and the U.S. Army Ranger School, and he served as a captain in the Field Artillery.